Con todo mi Amor
para Ti mi niña gratos
por ser tan especial
Que el 2006 sea un año lleno
de muchas Salud, Amor y abundancia de
Tu Amiga que te Adora y siempre
tiene presente

Feliz Navidad y Prospero año

Felicidad
Amor

RITUAL

By the same author:
Spirits of the Sacred Grove
Principles of Druidry
Thorsons Directions: D is for Druidry

RITUAL

A Guide to Life, Love and Inspiration

Emma Restall Orr
aka Bobcat

Thorsons

Thorsons
An Imprint of HarperCollins*Publishers*
77–85 Fulham Palace Road
Hammersmith, London W6 8JB

The Thorsons website address is: www.thorsons.com

Published by Thorsons 2000

3 5 7 9 10 8 6 4 2

© Emma Restall Orr 2000

Emma Restall Orr asserts the moral right to
be identified as the author of this work

A catalogue record for this book
is available from the British Library

ISBN 0 7225 3970 3

Printed and bound in Great Britain by Martins the Printers Ltd,
Berwick-upon-Tweed.

All rights reserved. No part of this publication may be
reproduced, stored in a retrieval system, or transmitted,
in any form or by any means, electronic, mechanical,
photocopying, recording or otherwise, without the prior
permission of the publishers.

This book I offer in thanks to Nic, without whom it would not have been written.
And with this offering of my creativity, I offer too of my strength ...
to laugh radiant at those sources of adolescent pain we have shared ...
to laugh in this torrent that is cleansing, healing rain ...
to laugh with affection, with each other, inspired.
Bless you.

CONTENTS

ACKNOWLEDGEMENTS

THE poems and prayers marked 'CG' throughout the book come from the *Carmina Gadellica*, translations by Alexander Carmichael with various adaptations. Those marked 'IM' are derived from Iolo Morgannwg's work. The Amergin poem in Chapter Four marked 'BL/PS' is a translation by Philip Shallcrass. Pieces marked 'BDO' are written by Philip Shallcrass and myself.

I would like to give thanks to Philip Shallcrass, Andrew Smith, Leslie Donaghy and Kate Ward for giving me invocations to their deities (Chapter Seven). The prayer marked 'SB' was given to the Gorsedd of the Isles of Britain by Septimus Bron (Chapter Ten).

I thank Denis Merrill for his inspiration, laughter, respect and irreverence.

I thank my husband, David, for the visions of his exquisite mind that took me down pathways I would not have found without him.

And I thank those who have gathered with me for the turning of the cycles, learning and celebrating with me, members of Tangwen's Grove, priestesses of the Dark Grove, all of the Gorseddau of the Isles of Britain, Philip, David and my family circle.

Thank you for your inspiration.

INTRODUCTION

I'M standing on the kerb in Fulham Palace Road, London, watching the traffic lights as cars snarl, crawling past me, in a haze of noise and exhaust pollution. A huge lorry growls as the traffic slows, letters in blue on the dirty grey of its side, and I wonder at the strangeness of a zebra crossing in such urban mayhem. It makes me smile. I look up to see a trio of starlings as they play beneath a dull grey sky.

Her words are lingering in my head.

'I was thinking about you writing a book on ritual.'

I find myself shaking my head and smiling, processing the ludicrous simplicity and impossibility of such a project. How could I find any validity for such a book within a tradition which has no liturgy and, at least in part, thrives for that very reason? How can I write another book about an oral tradition? For a moment I feel lost in the rumbling of the cars, my senses overwhelmed by the levels of sound, tangled by the constant movement all around me.

I close my eyes, feeling my feet on the pavement, reaching down through the concrete to find moist dark soil. The energy tingles in my soles, aiding my focus, as I draw it up through my body until my spirit is stretching into the cloudy skies. Above the traffic, a grey pigeon spreads his wings and hops from a high ledge into the air.

I turn to her, my editor. A smile from our conversation still touches her face and it broadens into a grin as the *beep-beep*ing of the lights tells us we can cross the road.

Later that day, in the humming tranquillity of the grove, I sit on an oak stump and watch as friends lay the fire. Old woodland stretches far enough in each direction to offer a sanctuary of seclusion and a priestess sings quietly to herself as she creates an altar on a flat log with roses, a loaf of home-baked bread, a chalice of wine. Smooth stones and seashells are arranged before it, a collection of feathers stuck into a knot of last year's barley, strands of ivy, leafy twigs of bay and oak. Four lanterns are lit and set beneath the oak trees at the edge of the glade.

It isn't just the beauty of what is being created here. If it were simply that, then its potency would not reach so deep. I watch warmth wash across the face of a young man as he steps into a stretch of sunlight, looking up towards its source, his whole body opening with thanks and ease. He's a schoolteacher; I know how much he's been needing the break.

A hand touches my shoulder.

'What are you dreaming, Bobcat?'

I smile, looking up into the face of an old friend. She crouches beside me.

'I was thinking about the book.'

We gaze at the fire as its first flames lick into the air, crackling through dry twigs of kindling, the blend of serenity and focus making it quite unnecessary to reply without pausing.

'What were you thinking?'

I sigh. 'I was wondering how to write about *this* ...'

THE SPIRIT

Two trees springing from one root without destruction.
A casket of poetry, an expression of wisdom.

The Colloquy of the Two Sages

what is
RITUAL?

 RITUAL. The word has been tumbling, turning slowly, through my mind. Pictures land around me, like dry autumn leaves. I frown, shake my head, and the images rise up and away in the breeze. I gaze at words as they slide inkily onto the page.

In the half light, I sink to my knees on the softness of the rug. I close my eyes, feeling the energy of my room as it moves around me, a gentle swirl, soundless and easy. I float on it, listening, not thinking, then take my mind sliding down through my spine, into the floor and through concrete to the dark mud beneath, to the rocks that are the bones of the earth, and there I lie back as she holds me, calm and still, spinning within this galaxy somewhere in space, in my room alone.

Opening my eyes, the spiral comes together, moving up through the sensitive nerves of my spine and, aware of my roots still anchored in the land, my body feels as light and free as if I had wings and the wind were beneath me. I reach with outstretched fingers to touch the white stone on the altar. It sparkles with tiny flakes of smooth sharp crystal. 'Hello,' I murmur.

My fingertips are warmed by it, glowing with it, though they hover just above its surface. Fire of the earth. A smile creeps through me, rising like a tide until it breaks across my face. 'So what *is* ritual?'

A BEGINNING

Ritual is the fine art of taking a break.

Pausing on this trodden path of everyday life, we give ourselves the time to see where we are walking. We delay our journey to gaze around, to contemplate, peruse and confirm our direction, to realize the extraordinary beauty and potential of the world around us.

It's experiential. A profoundly personal act even when shared, ritual reconditions our perspective. It is the practice of reminding ourselves of the value and power of living. It is that moment in which we stop and, looking around, understand that life is sacred.

THE SPIRIT

Perceiving the world as simply matter, as physical energy without purpose, as chemical reactions, doesn't take from it the miracle of its mechanics. The remarkable is all around us, pulsing within us. We needn't be walking paths cleared by an old religion or studying a spirituality to respect the powers of nature.

Yet shifting our point of perception to see the living energy of every creature, of every aspect of creation, transforms our world and the way we respond to it. This animistic view, which teaches us of the life force and allows the life force to teach us, acknowledges everything as being essentially of spirit. Spirit is the life force, the energy of creation. It is the centre point of any reality, the serene source and the intangible fire.

However much the flow of that energy comes of sentience, whatever the levels of consciousness and unconscious purpose, the physical form of every being is the creative expression of its spirit essence. The flowers of a clematis, dancing purple in the sunshine, reveal to us the beauty of its spirit nature, the energy that both shimmers within it and holds its form. The sheer silky colours of the python, moving with such focused ease, reflect the focus of its spirit. The bumble bee, the oyster, the oak, all show us faces of spirit, the energy of life flowing through creativity.

Pausing, stepping to one side, in the art of ritual, to see more clearly our journey and the pathway on which we walk, we learn to see the spirit essence. It is in that essence that the power of living lies.

 Ritual

THE SACRED

Creation, as an ongoing process, hums with the energy of becoming. Yet if all life is filled with the spirit of creation, how can we distinguish between what is sacred and what mundane?

Certainly it is possible to observe within the human soul what seems to me an innate craving for beauty, a need to find and hold on to objects we consider precious. The word 'sacred' is often defined as being the act of setting something aside, to be only used on certain days, kept in a safe and soft-lined box, literally or symbolically. In doing so, we hope to imbue it with longer life, with divine powers.

I consider 'sacred' to be a word enwrapped in the power of relationship. An object or creature, a person or place is sacred to us the moment we perceive its spirit, for in doing so we see the essence of its life force and the natural power of its creative potential. We see what connects it to the source of all life. Nothing that is perceived as sacred can ever be harmed or drained of energy except by those for whom it is simply matter. In seeing the spirit we honour the invulnerability that is the core of existence.

All creation is sacred because its essence is spirit. Yet what is sacred to us is limited by what we believe to be 'inspirited', what we perceive as spirit, consciously or subconsciously. To reach out and touch what is sacred is the foundation of all spirituality. Learning how to do this is the art of ritual.

SPIRIT TO SPIRIT

The sun is softly warm though the air is still cold, fresh with the early morning light of spring, and I walk slip-sliding in the dew-wet grass, the earth muddy from a week of endless rain. A robin perches on a tangled branch of bare hawthorn. He tilts his head, watching me carefully, listening to my footfalls in the grass. The horse grazing in the meadow lifts his head to watch me too, his breath cloudy in the chilly air as for a moment he waits, wondering. As I near the old ash, he turns away.

Walking softly, I touch the edge of the ash's naked canopy. Still sleepy with winter's cold, it's just starting to wake, stretching silently, reaching out to the tips

of its twigs with matt black leaf buds. In two months, when the buds are swollen to breaking, leaf clusters unfolding in pale green and early summer sun, the tide of its energy will be surging upwards, the sap rising, filling every vein of every bough and grey branch, the tiny twigs tingling with exquisite life as the whole tree sings in the dancing breeze. But now it yawns as I approach, settled in its still-ness, anticipating my tread upon the earth.

'May I join you?' I whisper.

There's a change in the light, as if the air had cleared a little, and I find myself drawn forward, conscious that I am walking now between the roots below me and the branches above. I have entered the private space of this tree I know so well and its energy shimmers through me. It is the most delicious embrace.

If something is sacred to us when we perceive its spirit, there is no need for us to set that thing aside as being too precious to handle. Far from it. Relating to the sacred inspires communication. In accepting that a tree, or bird or person, is filled with the creative force of life, we can craft a relationship with that individual on an entirely different premise from one that is not sacred. We don't dismiss the physical form of flesh and stone and wood, for that is the spirit's creativity, yet in seeing the spirit first we honour its power and beauty before reacting to the tangles of its temporal, mortal, linear reality.

Though we can acknowledge the spirit of a tree with our thinking minds, believing it to be so, perhaps even seeing the form of its energy, what we experience of that tree is limited to our thinking. If we were to see with our hearts, though, allowing ourselves a little vulnerability to sense and feel emotionally, what we would be able to share would deepen considerably.

Yet the greatest gift that we are offered in perceiving the world as sacred is the ability to see and hear, to breathe and dance, through the power of our own spirit. As spirit we are invulnerable, connected through the web of existence to all spirit; we are energy, vibrant and free, full with potential and patterned by natural purpose. As spirit our intuition about the physical world comes through our vision of matter being pliable, colourful and so intriguing. It is a resource, a palette, with which to manifest our soul's true and brilliant creativity.

 Ritual

SO, WHAT IS RITUAL?

Ritual is the act of pausing to learn on a journey that leads us to know that all life is sacred.

Certainty: Ritual affirms what we believe

Outside the swirling currents of everyday reality, the language of ritual is intensified by a focus without distraction. The words we use, our movements and gestures, whom we are speaking to and reaching to within that sacred space, all reflect the nature of our beliefs, both those we are aware of and those stored in the subconscious mind.

Within ritual we secure what we believe is true, asserting our perception, defining our expectation. What we don't believe exists, we are not likely to perceive. Where there is faith, a craving to believe, ritual guides that need to a place of knowing, grounding it, assuring us that it is real. Where our faith is deluded by fear and superstition, ritual steers us to understand this, offering us the strength and inspiration to release the need.

In clarifying our beliefs we create a certainty within. It's a lifelong process, ever flexible and changing, like the shifting sands of an ocean shore. If it becomes at all rigid or dogmatic, we block the fluidity of creation. Where simply it defines a stable footing for the next step to be taken, it brings confidence and the gentle serenity of knowing.

Congruence: Ritual is a tool for harmony

Once we have a sense of certainty, the art of ritual inspires us to find a synergy of intention. It offers us a time and place of perfect presence.

The beliefs we hold deep within us may be counter to what we are asserting. Though the stronger ones will guide our creativity, they may not be the positive or progressive, but rather keeping us defensive, shielding us against some threat of criticism or rejection.

The process and perspective of ritual directs us to the essence of our spirit's purpose, while acutely attuning to the changing world around us. In this way we are able to clarify our position and our direction, our inner and outer worlds sliding into an easy congruence.

With the stability of harmony, we look to the world around us.

Relationship: Ritual guides us to relate to spirit

Making a relationship, spirit to spirit, is an important part of the art of ritual. Not only are we affirming our perspective, honouring the individual – the new moon, the old oak tree, the person we love – as a sacred being, but we are also forging a time and place that is dedicated to developing and deepening the relationship further.

It may seem odd to speak of cultivating a relationship with a tree or spirit, but it is a process of discovery. Within ritual, we are able to explore the sacred, experiencing life through our own spirit energy and connecting with that of others. It is within that vision, connecting with spirit, that we are most filled with the creative energy of life. It is here that we find our inspiration, in the beauty and power of spirit's creativity.

Change: Ritual is a tool for transformation

The primitive drives of life are the ones that cause most mayhem, both within the individual psyche and within our society. These are the drives of survival, reproduction and familiarity.

Our survival instinct is played out through any actual or symbolic death, the need to hold on becoming entangled with an urge to release, to let go of the burden. In our culture we are seldom taught the craft of closure and death is barely spoken of, except in jest. The taboos confirmed by negative responses, death remains something to be feared, ignored or dismissed. Craving the ability to finish and leave, muddling that with the desire to abandon responsibility, we tiptoe around the issues, tangling the threads further.

The drive to reproduce is, of course, played out through sexuality, the dance of duality here being the games of attraction, of kiss and run, of yes and no, of surrender and control. Where the attracted couple are male and female, the complications are further muddied by the differences in mentalities; where the couple are of the same sex, further problems can arise from a non-comprehending heterosexual world. The sexual drive can be so strong, too, that we are faced with the complications of an animal instinct craving release through a self-consciously 'civilized' human mind.

Some say that the drive for familiarity is the strongest of all: we are liable to stay put in a dangerous or destructive situation simply because the fear of change looms larger than the 'devil we know'. Change can be terrifying. Opportunities are too often lost because the journey through is just too much to consider. The fear of change is the slippery mud on which we skid out of our sense of control, crashing through the barriers of our sanity.

Where ritual is used specifically to address those subjects that are difficult to deal with, particularly those clouded with social taboos such as sex, death and insanity, its power can be extraordinary. Ritual affords us a time and space for safely expressing deep emotion through periods of crisis and confusion.

When our perceptions are confused, tattered or wounded for any reason, the language of ritual offers us ways to reconnect with what heals, allowing us to clarify our beliefs, sort out the positive from the negative, and once again claim our strength. Asserting a clear perspective, spirit-conscious and compelling, ritual guides us in our need to understand the wild high tides of our souls' craving. Grounded in the here and now, it is a potent technique for facilitating and enabling any process of change, re-creating a world that is nourishing, body and soul.

Celebration: Ritual is a way of honouring change

Once change has been achieved, whether by ritual or by determination, celebrating is a critical part of the process. It affirms that the shift is done, declares it openly to those who would witness it, and closes the gate to ensure that reversing is not an option.

Celebration within ritual allows us to do this while still relating on a spirit to spirit level. Here we are able to give thanks where it is due, strengthening our relationship with those who have inspired us. Here we can find our joy, held within the magical moment of the ritual space, exploring our soul's wild creativity unhampered by inhibitions. In doing so, we learn more deeply the value of laughter, pleasure and delight, spirit to spirit, sacred and free.

THIS BOOK

This book, then, is about ritual as a spiritual practice, a medium of communication, a language of words and actions that allows us to express our perception of spirit, of our world as sacred, and to interact with that world. Ritual is an effective way of affirming the positive, of processing and creating change, of strengthening our connection with the world around us and our consciousness of ourselves as spirit beings. Ritual is a dance of our spirit's creativity as we manifest our reality and celebrate its beauty.

My own understanding of ritual, the language I use, is inspired by the old British tradition of Druidry. In the next chapter, we can explore what that means and how it has shaped my vision.

Ritual

what is
DRUIDRY?

HALF A DOZEN CLIPS

When I discovered the tradition was still alive, somewhere in the mid-1980s, images of Druids were still most often limited to the mythic stereotype – an old man with a long white beard and robes of white linen, who walked with an ornate staff and kept a sharp golden sickle tucked into a pocket, just in case he should happen across an oak bearing mistletoe while serenely wandering the paths of the forest.

For a good deal of the last decade, the pixie inside me has enjoyed how utterly I don't fit into that image. Of course, the physical form of the stereotype is a superficial glaze, but it does act for many as a signpost, evoking a sense of recognition, inviting you, 'Come on, step a little closer.' The image took me back to my childhood superhero, Getafix, the Gaulish Druid of the *Asterix* cartoons who had so intrigued me, stirring my imagination into hours of playing out dreams. Roaming the old forests, watching waltzing butterflies, finding fat mushrooms, catching the scent of foxes in the softness of the breeze, I walked beside Getafix, sat and listened to his teachings about herbs and stars and magical brews.

Fifteen years later, in my early twenties, it was the extraordinary blend of Getafix's invincibility and human vulnerability that I had loved so much as a child, his power and tenderness, which drew me back to Druidry. My thirst dragged me stumbling through all the books I could find. Some were wonderful mythic tales, some so boring my eyes watered with stupor. Time and again I kept crashing into the walls of a dead end, another path having taken me to a place I couldn't recognize, a place too rigidly coloured by the image of a stern old man.

Slowly the model of the Druid has been changing. As more people find their own way into the tradition, their energy and perceptions have shifted the stereotype into a modern guise, one which is both accessible to men and to women, and yet still holds the essence of the 'old man in white'.

Let me offer a few images of modern Druidry.

A young man, his eyes closed, sits on the thickened grey roots of an old beech. His head is tilted a little to one side, swaying as if to a rhythm he hears inside. He frowns, tensing, moving a little forward, as though hoping to hear more clearly the subtleties of a melody, and a smile touches his lips. Half opening his eyes, he reaches into the pocket of his jacket, moving his feet an inch or so, his walking boots digging very slightly into the muddy ground, and he lifts the tin flute to his mouth, closing his eyes again, breathing in as if he were preparing to sigh. He starts to play, and as the notes rise in the soft autumn sunshine another leaf comes drifting down, almost weightless in the hint of a breeze.

In a large, wide and iron-black dish, open beneath the night's dark sky, a fire burns with orange-gold flickering flames only occasionally breaking through the crust of ashen wood. A lick of yellow heat reaches up, as if playing surreptitiously, as four women move without a sound, their bodies swaying, twitching, tensing, then floating again as if the chilly wind were warm dark water. Around them are stones, chunks of rock, some lying, some standing, each one watching, listening to the women, to the humming, the toning that seeps from their souls, as they invoke through their reverence the dark mother of creation, their goddess of winter.

On a burial mound some miles away, some hours later in the half light of dawn, a man wrapped in a cloak of wolf pelts and the damp and sparkling weight of dew, his eyes open wide, his arms reaching for the skies, alone relives the pain of an ancestor long dead, calling silently through his exhilaration for some divine guidance. A buzzard glides through the valley below, gazing with such focus, held on the wind.

Ritual

Crows pass by beneath the pale grey sky. Words tumble from the man's lips. The story must be told, whoever is listening.

In the daylight, before work, a woman walks out into her garden, her feet crunching on dry leaves upon the grass. Her fingers brush against the foliage of a yew, as if with affection, as she makes her way towards the altar. A bundle of dark red flowers is clasped in her fingers. She bows as she approaches. 'Hail spirits,' she whispers. A frown she is barely aware of creases the skin of her brow. As she lays the blooms on the old granite plinth, the flower maiden smiles, her stone face adjusting its focus to peruse the energy before her. The woman feels it. For a moment she closes her eyes and makes her prayers. On her way back to the house, she picks a blackberry from the hedge, squeezing it between her fingers, touching her smiling lips with its dark red juice.

A candle flame hesitates, for a moment wondering whether or not to withdraw back into darkness. He watches as it breathes in deeply and stretches into the energy of the room, and he nods his thanks, almost perceptibly, sitting back on the ashwood meditation stool. The long white robe hangs by the door, waiting until he is ready, and he turns to the altar, bringing his consciousness softly into balance. The ceremony will be challenging, remembering the words, keeping the flow clear and directed, contained, yet already he can feel the anticipation of it being done. As he slips back to presence, the shimmering of his life force tingles in the tips of his fingers.

The wind is wet with misty rain and surf. Though oblivious to the man jogging past her, his dog panting, racing by his side, she is aware of the marks her shoes leave in the sand and the weight of her robe, dark indigo velvet, getting heavier, wetter. The hum of the seagull feathers tied into her hair, playing in the wind as if taunting it, hovers in her ears, screaming in a whisper, 'Set me free, if you can, if you can, set me free!' And gently her voice rises up from within her, calling to the old goddess of the waves that wash the shore, until all she hears are the melodies intermingling, her own voice and the waves singing, as she calls for inspiration, her spirit dancing with her hair and the feathers in the wind.

Images of individuals ... They include a teacher, a shop owner, a computer technician, an artist, a lawyer and a psychotherapist, though probably not in the order that you'd expect. A few of them belong to Druid groups; most work in Groves (the term used for a group of Druids who celebrate together). This excerpt of their lives reveals a living, breathing spirituality, in six contrasting shades of its diversity.

AN ORAL TRADITION

Druidry is and always has been an oral tradition. Little has been passed down – no brown brittle pages of age-old rituals, no prayer books of devotions or scriptures of law. What writings we do have contain no perfect clarity, for they are stories and poems, myths and tales of war, each one rich with imagery, love and realization, pain and inspiration, yet none offering us certainty. Indeed, as an oral tradition, it is recognized that any tale told anywhere in life, even those declared to be true historical fact, is a tale well coloured and embellished by the teller's own perceptions and opinions.

Inspiration there is in the old tales, nonetheless, both in the writings of the Classical historians and philosophers and in our own medieval literature. Folklore and ballads teach us yet more. Yet to search out a validity for modern Druidry by trawling through old writings is to misunderstand the spirit of the tradition. I cannot claim that the rituals in this book are 'authentic ancient Druidry', nor would I want to; such a creature no longer exists and if it did, it would be utterly unsuited to modern life. Druidry, as an oral tradition, has existed and survived like a river flowing through time, evolving with the changing landscape of each dawning day.

By looking underneath the white robes of the old Druid (if you'll excuse the innuendo), we can see the essence of his power, his ability to exude the invulnerable force of his spirit through the tender temporality of his human creativity and physicality. Indeed, it is by looking beneath the practice of modern Druidry, between the words of the old texts, reaching into the gaps, that we find the essence of the tradition. It is by following the river to its spring source that we can taste its purity and its power.

ANCIENT ROOTS

The old writings clearly state that the tradition emerged in Britain. Students of two millennia past travelled to these islands to learn its wisdom, a wisdom inspired by the diversity of this landscape, its changing and temperate climate shaping its being, together with the influence of the many cultures that have settled here over millennia. Like the breath of life, it was – and still is – drawn in by the people and exhaled, to be drawn in by the trees and exhaled. Like the soil itself, it is created of our ancestors' lives, the decayed matter breaking down to become this fertile earth, nourishing them then as it nourishes us now.

The earliest clearly discernible traces of spirituality in these lands are the tomb shrines. What ritual took place at these sites we can only imagine, but it is clear that the focus was on the power of death. Around 5,000 years ago, as the population grew and agriculture became established, the focus shifted to the power of fertility. Stone circles were built as calendars or sacrificial sites, sanctified places in which peoples could gather to declare social changes, witness vows and transactions. Still the powers of nature were revered, with the priests given the role of reaching to the forces that directed those powers, making pleas, offering gifts of appeasement and searching for understanding.

With 99 per cent of our DNA still that of the hunter-gatherer, not so very much has changed in the human psyche through these 6,000 or 7,000 years of civilization. The wild forces of death and survival, sex and fertility, and the spinning energy of change, are still the elements that underpin our lives, and those that we do all we can to tame.

CELTIC BRITAIN

A shift in climate a millennium or so before the common era brought many long centuries of wet weather, turning the spiritual focus in Britain towards the power of the water gods, with burials and sacrifice, offerings and shrines revering the forces of nature that dwelled in the rivers, birthing life through the springs, bringing the rain.

When the Iron Age culture that emerged within central Europe spread across to Britain around 500 BCE, ideas spread as fluently and quickly as trade. With the technology of charcoal and the smelting of iron came all the associated wit and strength, offering a new kind of speed and violence in war that leaked into the cultures who used its power. This is the period of the so-called Celts, a term given to the Europeans of the period just a few hundred years ago by historians, romantics and early archaeologists, despite there being little cohesion amongst tribal peoples of the era.

Just as agriculture and hunting would have differed region to region, spirituality was also still an intensely localized affair. It is unlikely that there were any deities revered all across Europe, though from our retrospective standpoint it isn't hard to find common attributes and linguistic links that suggest it. Deities were those of this mountain and that meadow, of the valley's wind, the summer storm clouds, of the river and the mist, the wild boar of the forest. The rituals needed and performed would have been equally diverse.

It is in the Roman literature that we first find the word 'Druid' used to describe the spiritual élite of Britain and Gaul. How long this priesthood had used that particular term to describe themselves, we can have no idea.

When the Roman armies arrived in these islands, their spiritual tradition was similar to that of the British they encountered: a European paganism that honoured the gods of the earth, the seas and skies, together with the gods of their homelands and their ancestors. Focused on wealth and trade, not religious confrontation, it was their demand for the political power that was held by the Druids that led to the fragmentation of the native tradition. Those Druids who co-operated, sharing their knowledge, both teaching and learning from the Romans, worked within the new order. Those who didn't were persecuted and killed as a blended Romano-British culture emerged.

Pagan Roman rule brought to the native religion a civilizing effect, temples and shrines being crafted now of carved stone, the priests being paid in coins for the first time. Though it easily incorporated influences from the many tribes conscripted into the Roman armies, it was no less a localized spirituality. Gods and spirits of the vicinity were honoured beside the ancestral gods of the newcomers, as they had always been.

Archaeology and writings of the period give us clear if scant details of a religious and spiritual philosophy and practice from this time, including the names of native deities that might otherwise have been lost. A good deal of modern Druidry finds inspiration in these snippets of information.

THE LAST 1,500 YEARS

With the end of Roman rule, Britain slid back to a simpler mud and wattle reality, the stability of the previous centuries quickly disappearing beneath the turbulence of more violent raiders and settlers. When the chieftains were presented with the image of a powerful war god, a religion that was moving through politically successful peoples, they took on its banner. So Christianity became another invading force, working its way slowly through the people but quickly becoming a part of the political attitude of the governing classes.

It made as much of an impact on the old spirituality of these islands as it has done on native and indigenous traditions all over the world. Walking in with blinkers of evangelical self-assertion, dishonouring the spirits of the land upon which it walked, dismissing deity in any other form but that of its own, it was a political invasion. Bringing a mountain-desert god of the Middle East, it was used as a tool of control, breaking apart the peoples' connections with the spirits of their land, the elemental forces around them, the powers of the natural world on which they were dependent. Such a mentality has little to do with mystical spiritual Christianity, but its effects are obvious in our current environmental crisis.

For 1,500 years, the pagan spirituality and religion of Druidry fought to survive, coming up against dwindling tolerance as folk customs were suppressed, the old myths forgotten, the people losing their bond with nature. The invading bands of Saxons and Danes brought with them a fresh input of pagan perspectives, fighting the Christianized Romano-British kings, but they were the last before the Norman conquerors established an oppressive and monotheistic rule. Elements of the Saxon and Nordic cultures can still be found in Druidry today.

Through the following centuries, the old traditions of Druidry survived mainly through the Bardic Colleges, some of which remained in existence until the

mid-eighteenth century. Magical, spiritual and creative practices were taught – divination, sacrifice, the arts of poetry.

Antiquarianism, a forerunner to archaeology, emerged as classical literature found new translations, inspiring a new interest in medieval insular (British and Irish) texts and a new interest in Druidry. From this evolved what is now known as the Druid revival of the eighteenth century. Created essentially by a male leisured class searching for a spiritual philosophy that was solar oriented yet monotheistic, it embraced a fantasy that Druidry had been a preparation for Christianity. Its rituals were formal and highly structured, its groups hierarchical and intellectual.

There are Druid orders still in existence which date back to this period and hold much of its colour and texture even now. Indeed, the figure of the white-robed Druid was born at this time, one image of many in the Classical literature being adopted in preference to others. The notion of a Druid in red or black didn't quite inspire the old men as they pondered the noble wisdom of their spiritual ancestors ...

PAGANISM AND TOLERANCE

In the 1960s, the philosophies of paganism began to re-emerge and by the mid-1980s Druidry was established once again as an animistic and polytheistic tradition, closer to what it had been before the invasion of political monotheism. Yet, as in any tradition that accepts the reality of many gods, Druidry is an inclusive and eclectic spirituality which does not seek to dismiss any other tradition.

The population of India was of countless different spiritualities, each religious focus and philosophy being shaped by its natural context. It was the British who brought these traditions under one banner, calling it Hinduism, a term simply meaning 'the people of the Indus valley'. Druidry exists in just the same way, holding within it the religious threads that come of many different environments and ancestral lines. Like Hinduism, it is philosophically pagan; the word 'pagan', if translated from the Latin *paganus*, taking into account the social and cultural context of the word, can be accurately and simply defined as 'the honouring of the spirits of one's locality', as opposed to looking primarily to government as the ruling power. Like any native tradition such as Huna, Shinto and Asatru, or the spiritualities of the Aborigine and Maori, Native American and African peoples, Druidry has been coloured by the landscape and climate of its home environment.

It is to some extent, however, more complex than purely pagan traditions, for it is a spiritual philosophy that is of value to some despite their practice within monotheistic or humanistic traditions. For example, within Druidry there are Christians and Jews who accept a philosophical paganism – honouring the land and the ancestors as aspects of divine and sacred creation – yet who revere one god in their religious practice.

It is normal in Druidry not often to mention the names of the gods, there being an assumption that one may not know which deity another reveres. Traditional blessings or vows use words such as, 'in the names of your gods and the gods of your ancestors'. The oldest recorded states, 'I swear by the gods my people swear by', giving away no clues as to who those might be ...

A NATIVE SPIRITUALITY

Druidry is, then, the natural native spirituality of what were once called the Pretannic Isles. 'Britain' derives from this ancient word, which means 'the islands of the Painted People', referring to both Britain and Ireland. As any other native tradition, it strives to listen to the earth and the ancestors, recognizing them as teachers.

Yet, though it is inspired by a particular landscape, it is not captive to that place. In Druidry it is understood that, wherever we walk, we take with us all that has made us what we are, our ancestors of blood and of our spiritual and cultural heritage; at the same time, we must always acknowledge and honour the land beneath our feet, and all those who inspirit it. So it is that we weave the threads of who we are and where we are, retaining an awareness of the present and our presence within it.

Ritual in the Druid tradition is intrinsically focused on this sacred weave. Calling with reverence and respect to the 'spirits of place' and to the ancestors, asking that both inspire, bless, guide, protect and witness the ceremony that is to take place, the sacred space is created.

It is with this understanding, too, that Druidry has spread across the world, as people find inspiration in its spiritual philosophy and nourishment in its practice. Some follow the threads of their ancestry back to the Pretannic Isles, celebrating their Druidic faith while honouring the spirits of the land on which they now live. Others, newly come to these shores, find inspiration in the land, yet know too that to honour it they need not abandon the gods of their own people.

THE FLOW OF LIFE

Druidry, then, is a natural spirituality of our culture, having evolved through the millennia that people have lived on these islands. It is wrapped in the soft mists of spring, woken by the summer storms, nourished by the falling leaves of autumn, touched by the kiss of winter frost. It speaks with the energy of the moors and the meadows, whispering with the wind in the ancient oaks, gliding with the buzzards high over the rocky peaks, humming the waggle dance with the bumble bees.

Its inherent simplicity asks only for an acknowledgement of the natural world, the land that feeds us, those who gave us life, and within that is created a sanctified place from which we might reach to the gods, whosoever they may be, to give thanks for life and love.

It is the flow of life that is the power of nature and that which draws us into the tradition, guiding us within it. Its spirals and streams that are the cycles and tides of life, waxing and waning, receding and flooding out again, ever creating, are the exquisite sources of inspiration that are so quested in the tradition.

In the next chapter we'll look more closely at this flow of inspiration, beginning to explore how it lies at the heart of ritual practice.

Ritual

sources of INSPIRATION

THE SOUL'S CRAVING

There is a part in each one of us which seems to take pleasure in evading satisfaction – bizarre, perhaps, but behaviour that allows us to avoid the risks involved, for in the reaching out for satisfaction we face the danger of falling short and landing heavily in the mud. Aching with an inner hunger, we live with that basic human paradigm which asserts that we are simply not 'good enough', a belief which protects us from failure and rejection by constraining our creativity, maintaining that we don't deserve abundance and satisfaction.

The extraordinary power of love, when the chemicals are fizzing and the sense of soul recognition is quite overwhelming, can appease that hunger, removing an underlying loneliness, a fear of isolation. However, even if the relationship thrives and the love grows, it requires more than just knowing the other soul to satisfy that elusive craving.

Finding a solution to the problem of lack of fulfilment is a driving force in many lives. Numbing it with alcohol and drugs is one way to address it. Quick-fix explosions of adrenalin or lust, and complex distractions like overwork and obsession, are all answers, though neither healthy nor effective. The wanting in our souls niggles all the more, digging deeper whenever we try to ignore it.

SOUL CREATIVITY

Yet occasionally we come across people who, brimming with life, seem utterly satisfied. They may be corporate CEOs or simply growing sweet peas, deep sea photographers or full-time mothers; it matters not how glamorous and successful society might perceive them to be. What they have found is a sense of their own creativity. Some may have stumbled perchance upon the opportunity, while others may have struggled for years, making mistakes along the way until something brought them to just the right doorway.

I believe that not only is finding a creative outlet an essential part of good living – and Druidic philosophy affirms this entirely – but the creativity that truly feeds us is actually more specific than simply a particular medium. As unique as we are in our idiosyncratic individuality, our soul creativity is very specific: a style, a distinct subject, a particular forum. We are specializing creatures in a tribal mentality, searching for a place where our particular talents can be acknowledged. Our soul craves that opportunity and only when it comes can the spirit's deep creative energy flow without hesitation, rewarding us with the exhilaration of both freedom and identity.

For many that place is not yet found. Some glimpse it but shy away, nervous of the power of potential it exudes. Perhaps the inspiration needed just hasn't arrived. Inspiration – that beautiful moment when it all falls into place, when we know suddenly what to do and how to do it, and the vision is fuelled with all the energy required.

Except that, by its very nature, inspiration is erratic (or so we are led to believe in a secular culture). It hits us like lightning, searing out of the blue, out of our control.

Druidry sees it differently.

THE SEARCH FOR INSPIRATION

This search for inspiration is at the very heart of Druidry. If we were to sum up the Christian tradition in one word, it might be 'salvation'; to do the same with Druidry, the word would be 'inspiration'. Both express the focus of the quest, the energy of life that fills the Holy Grail, the crystal waters of the eternal spring, the sweet scent and warm milk of Mother Earth.

The imagery of the Grail, the sacred container of the elixir of life, is common to so many traditions. As ancient cauldron within which the gods concoct their magical brews, it holds the wisdom of perfect knowledge, of rebirth or eternal life, of soul-deep healing. As chalice, it holds the essence of divinity, the sacred blood of the sacrificed deity or king. The search for the Grail is not for a cup, but for a draught of pure inspiration. So what is this inspiration?

The creative life force, it enters us as a hit of clear and brilliant energy. Bypassing the protective-defensive beliefs that hold us so constrained, it is a waking shout of shattering clarity that reveals a vision of true potential. So it is that, when we aren't struggling to find a solution, when we are distracted and riding another current of thought, inspiration has a chance to slip in through the barricades.

With this understanding, the Druid knows that it is possible to have inspiration 'on tap'. Instead of waiting, wishing powerlessly, hoping desperately for a break, it is possible to find ways of accessing that flow of clear life energy whensoever we wish. Questing the Grail need not be a blind task, and once tasted, when we know what it is to be filled with the energy of such strong exquisite clarity, our life turns to one focus: to taste it again. Suddenly at our fingertips we have the ability to explore our soul creativity, the only remedy that brings the gift of fulfilment.

AWEN

In the British tradition of Druidry, *awen* is a Welsh word poetically translated as 'sacred inspiration'. Literally, it means 'flowing spirit' and it is the essence of life, the creative energy streaming through the currents and tides of living. It is the bubbling birthing water of the spring, the passion of love, the wild laughter of the wind. It has been interpreted as 'poetic frenzy'; it is the energy that passes between artist and muse.

In Druidic perception, where the world is vital and vibrant with the energy and wisdom of the sacred, and textured, coloured, formed with the creativity of spirit, *awen* is understood to flow as the essence of spirit to spirit relationship. It is the touch of the sky gods upon the Earth and the earth's opening, giving response; it is the kiss of lightning, the explosion of conception, the eruption of germination. It is the electric charge of soul to soul recognition.

Acknowledging the sacred, honouring the spirit with wonder and respect, we begin to form a relationship, be it with a mountain, a tree, the moon or another human, slowly understanding the power of our own spirit as our perception of the spirit before us heightens and clarifies. Relationship is about reaching further and, being open, allowing the energy of another to touch us, spirit to spirit, and to respond. That exchange of sacred energy is an experience of ecstasy, clarity, affecting us body, heart and soul. It is the communion of *awen*, a sharing of life's essence. Some might say this is a definition of love.

FINDING INSPIRATION

Spirits of the natural world, the stones and rocks, plants and trees, the moon and stars, the streams and oceans, bugs and bees and scampering beetles, the feathered and furry and silky soft creatures, our children and our lovers, ancestors long dead and those who linger in our memories, the colours and scents and the laughter and tears, flying, running, sleeping, gliding, each one offering the creativity of its spirit as fire and flesh and leaf and waterdrop, each one inspires. Where any spirit expresses its creativity, there is a source of inspiration.

Because each individual is working with different ancestral lines, perceiving his own environment in a different way, the earth beneath his feet, the colours and textures of the skies, the tides of the ocean that salts the air, each person finds his inspiration in different guises. Sometimes it is in the energy and power of spirit itself, but more often we glimpse the *awen* in the spirit's creativity. In the music we hear the composer's life energy flowing. In the soft petals of the rose we see the spirit's *awen*.

In the Druidry of past generations, inspiration was sought in various ways. Teasing out ideas, exploring the mind, discovering what was effective, our ancestors pushed themselves to the edges of life. Using sensory deprivation, toxins and trance, deep sleep and sleeplessness, fear and beauty, empathy and isolation, music and love, the stories and poetry of our land were created.

Though many of these techniques are tricks of intention and distraction, the key is always in relationship and sacred vision, the spirit to spirit exchange. Searching our souls at the outskirts of endurance and sanity, new insights can flood over us, yet without such drastic measures, simply in the course of waking to the sacred that inspires us, we work to secure the flow of inspiration. Finding the connection or recognition (however one-sided that may initially be), turning to face it, we commit ourselves to developing it.

We may consider that the beauty of the moon in a dark sky, shining white with the light of the sun reflected, shimmering rainbows in halos of atmospheric moisture, is a sharing of many spirits' creativity. Yet so is all creation, a weaving of threads of energy and intent, direct and reflected. Every relationship is based on both individuals' vision of each other, and relationship is the key: connecting, communicating, sharing, spirit to spirit, the power and energy that is life.

Of course, some folk, be they stones, creatures or people, however beautiful they may seem to be, however much they give us simply by being what they are, shining with their own existence, aren't interested in forming any kind of a relationship. It may be that we sense their rebuff, yet our mistake may simply be that we have approached in the wrong way, clumsily or blindly being offensive or frightening. It may be that whatever we were to give, the spirit would turn away anyway, and this must be respected.

THE GODS

Where pagan spiritual philosophy slips into religious practice, the most potent forces of nature are revered as deities. Pouring energy into the environment, creating the hills and rivers, thunder and mist, the wind and the forest, the frosts and the moon, these are the 'spirits of place', the powers of the environment within which we live.

When a tribe leaves its homeland to settle elsewhere, if the spirits and powers of nature have been strong for the people, they will take their reverence for those gods along with their memories. These gods then become the ancestral gods, holding the energy of the people, the gods of a tribe and its tides of emotion, guiding its creativity.

Ancestral gods have sometimes travelled so far from their origin in both time and space that any understanding of their expression as powers of nature has been lost. Still holding the energy, though, these gods exist within the flows of emotion, of love and war, knowledge and passion. The energy of our primitive drives – survival, sexuality and familiarity – emerging through the cycles of life, death, love and rebirth, is held by these old gods of the dark valleys, wild storms and deserts, mountains, meadows and life-giving springs.

While it may be hard to build a relationship with a deity, it brings such exquisite reward that the costs are often readily paid. The exchange of energy that is the communion of spirit floods the body and soul with brilliant inspiration. Whether that deity is a god of love or a goddess of sexuality, a god of thunder or a goddess of the wildwood, whatever power of nature is held by that force, the *awen* that flows will be of that same quality. Using different sources of inspiration according to what is needed for our soul creativity is a part of the journey, the quest for *awen*.

In the tradition as I was taught it, various techniques of reaching inspiration were explored, including many of the old ways, some of which will be explained further on in this book. The basis was nonetheless always the same: honouring an expression of creativity with deep respect, reaching into the source of that power with reverence, listening, watching, forming a relationship, spirit to spirit, and sharing the pleasure of the connection that is the flow of inspiration.

WORKING WITH THE NEGATIVE

Where negative beliefs block our ability to receive or perceive the sacred and share energy on this level, we are denied access to inspiration. Yet where beauty in creativity evokes wonder, allowing us naturally and easily to lose ourselves in experiencing it, a pathway is made that bypasses the negative, filling us with life. Deepening our connection with the source of beauty and creativity, this source of *awen*, bringing ourselves back to that place again and again, exploring it and exploring how it makes us feel, can be a poignant and effective way of breaking down negative beliefs.

Where the flow of life energy isn't strong enough, either because the blocks of self-negation are still slowing it down or the relationship is not yet as firm as it

could be, *awen* can pour in and be quashed by negativity, suffocating the creativity. By strengthening the relationship, however, inspiration can and does act as a powerful tool of processing, cleansing the mind and pouring its energy into that which brings positive feedback, nourishing the soul on its journey to freedom.

Yet inspiration does not always come through beauty and joy. When negativity has not closed our vision of nature's power altogether, the wounds and emotional traumas of living can also open doorways to inspiration. Some of the greatest art and poetry has been crafted with the *awen* of a desperately painful soul to soul relationship.

Difficult negative emotion can be seen as the autumn and winter of the mind's cycles, naturally breaking down our internal environment, offering the lore of decay and death before the spring and summer of growth. But where there is a sense of self, a vision of the sacred, suffering need not be a part of the experience of such emotional tides.

Creativity expressed from the inspiration of negative emotion can be challenging, continuing a course of breakdown and decay. Yet when the *awen* is glowing in it, albeit black and snarling, it can be inspiring to others and their positive response can halt the soul's crisis. Finding beauty in creativity born of negative emotion is an important part of healing, both in terms of individual suffering and in humanity as a whole.

CREATIVE CYCLES

Creating any relationship is about sharing ideas and energy in whatever way seems appropriate. Without the exchange, relationship breaks down – or never gets started. When we are working on a sacred level, the basics are just the same.

While inspiration may tag us when we aren't looking, accessing it consciously requires us to trust enough to receive the flow. In the vulnerability of being naked to the soul, conscious of our physical creativity, conscious of our spirit, we reach out to make contact, breathing deeply of the source. Yet, filled with the energy, the insight and beauty, our insecurity can provoke us to clutch on to its power, and holding any energy within us, be it love, anger, calories or inspiration, can be unhealthy. That energy must be expressed in the same way that inhaling must be followed by exhaling, or we will swell with it, becoming blocked and weighed down. This cycle of inspiration and creative expression is an integral part of living life in a sacred manner.

In Druidry, we offer our creativity as a gift to the spirit that inspired us. This act can be simply sitting on the beach at sunset, watching the sun sinking into the dark water, reading the poem that was written inspired by the same scene a few days before. It can be an offering given within the consecrated circle of intricate ceremony, calling to the spirit that inspired with dedications and commitments, the affirmation of actions and changes. It can be the ritual of presenting food blessed and made with love to the person who has inspired you with so much love.

Offerings made to the sources of inspiration establish and nurture the relationship, so we give our gifts of creativity in the hope that they will be inspiring to the other spirit, whether it appears in the form of a tree, a person or cat, or shimmering with the potent energy of deity. As the relationship develops, so our ability to receive the flow of inspiration grows, and the cycles of life, grounded in physical creativity, spiral higher and higher into freedom.

LOVE

Relationship is the key to finding inspiration 'on tap'. Creating a bond by honouring the spirit, exploring levels of trust, intimacy and sharing, we break out of a mentality that is tight with threat and competition. Recognizing spirit, seeing the sacred, respecting the flow of life, we open ourselves to receive its exquisite stream of *awen*.

To define love is a quandary of semantics that is liable to get entangled in every person's need to believe life is a certain way. Some say that if it hurts it isn't love but need. Yet most of us declare a relationship to be one of love even when there are issues of conditional exchange, expectation, dependence, compromise and all the other brittle intricacies that so easily can snap and leave us hurting.

Perceiving the spirit of the one we love – person, cat, tree, mountain, moon – and learning to relate on that level, conscious of the tides of inspiration and creativity that flow between us, gives us the vision to understand more clearly the nature of a love that doesn't hurt. It is a long journey, but glimpses of this exquisite reality can be a scent to follow on our human adventure that is life.

Discovering ways of creating an environment within which it feels safe to make the first tentative and tender steps is an important part of the process. To be kicked back by negative feedback, failure and disappointment can be brutally devastating, particularly when we are dealing with issues that do touch us deeply like love, trust and relationship. The art of ritual is a medium that offers us a language of patterns, imagery and belonging, giving us the sense of security we need in order to take the risks and make the changes.

SO...

RITUAL

is a pause in time, a break from the tumbling swirls and eddies of life's river. It gives an opportunity to check our beliefs, both those that are sound and those that need to be changed. It reveals the world as sacred, guiding us to relate more closely to its creativity and its essence, to understand more respectfully the spirit of nature, its power and potential.

DRUIDRY

is a spirituality rooted deeply in the land yet responding anew to each dawning day. A tradition that honours our environment, the internal and external worlds, the spirits of the earth, sea and skies, the spirits of our ancestors, it is a philosophy that has within it the exploration of sacred relationship, spirit to spirit.

INSPIRATION

is the flow of life energy that *is* the changing, growing, fruiting, dying nature of creation, called in Druidry *awen*. It is possible to access this flow consciously, to use its power as a way of enthusing life, of finding freedom and freeing love.

Having explored the foundational ideas, the earth underfoot, in the next section of this book we'll look at the framework of ritual within which these ideas can be used. Knowing a little of the mud and stones that make up the path, let us then walk on into the sacred grove ...

THE SANCTUARY

If you go into the forest for a day
take bread for a week.

Irish proverb

the language of
RITUAL

COMMUNICATION

Wherever there is a sense of threat, a fear of scarcity, whether of land or water, food or safety, security or love or approval, there is the competition that breeds on such a fear, inciting cravings for a clenched power that dominates and denigrates. The response to this looming autocratic shadow of poverty, violence and disease, immorality, rejection, is the countering authority of human politics. Where one person is seen to represent the oppressing force, the focus of blame is swiftly piled upon them.

Yet good living is cultivated through individual relationships, person to person, where neither party is projecting any vision of threat or dominance on the other, where a language is found that can be mutually understood. Miracles of peace, community, abundance and healing are achieved simply by the forging of soul to soul relationships.

When we are interacting with the world as sacred, the needs are the same. It is not unusual for someone to assume that there is risk when looking to a force of nature, when sensing the energy of a forest, knowing the potential of the storm, glimpsing the power of the muse. If we perceive these as deity, the tendency is often to perceive them as a dominant authority and to slide into submission and/or resentment in response.

Yet spirit to spirit there is no threat. There is dissimilarity, increasingly so as we move from the core of life energy towards the spirit's creativity in manifest form. There is a contrast in strength between the hurricane and the mouse in terms of the physical impact each might have on the oak. But in a sacred world the flows of inspiration might tell quite a different story.

If ritual is a time and space in which we can learn how to craft stronger relationships, it is also in ritual that we can learn the language of sacred communication. Stepping out of the currents of life to explore our truth, we are offered an opportunity to re-create ourselves as better reflections of that truth.

Responding from that place of naked honesty is a slow process of discovering trust and understanding the spirit. We search for perfect words, for lines of poetry, for ancient prayers and invocations. We try sound and music, breaking the inhibitions of the physical body with drama and with dance. We retell ancestral stories and the tales of our own lives; we try using the mundane talk of daily reality. We craft exquisite implements and create beautiful interplay with props and tools, and without doubt all of these play an important part in the creative art of our ritual. Yet it needs more.

Druid ritual is a play of sacred relationship, where we are perceiving spirit and, in the process, reaching for consciousness of our own core. What it requires is a form of communication that does not remain dissociated from material existence. We need to (a) touch the spirit; (b) fully understand; and (c) let the lessons pour through into flesh and mud.

THREE LEVELS

To spirit, committed intention is all

Coming to a realization about some issue, knowing and declaring that some act must be done, making the decision to offer a gift, to affirm a commitment deep within the soul, to honour spirit, we set our minds upon a ritual.

If our intention is strong, clear and directed, its energy will immediately be felt humming across the web of spirit, touching all those who are involved. For spirit, the power of intention is the focus above all else.

Matching beliefs and intention, we find the energy of expression

However clear our intention, there may be deep in our subconscious minds powerful assumptions and attitudes that contradict it – and that will undermine any attempts we make to change. Without an awareness of what is blocking our progress, the process can be increasingly demoralizing.

The adventures of self-exploration that wake us to these protective and constraining beliefs is a critical part of any journey to freedom and the art of ritual is an effective practice along the way. As ritual is performed, our awareness of underlying patterns and expectations grows, together with our perception of a sacred world. Our intention might shift, adjusting to the new knowledge, or it may be confirmed, strengthened with resolve.

While the spotlight of our consciousness will respond to thought, the subconscious uses a language of energy. Understanding movement, dance and gesture, colour and sound, imagery and symbolism, the subconscious is touched by anything that evokes a flow of energy, emotional and physical, laughter and love, fear and anger, wonder and joy.

As the aims of our thinking self and those of the inner mind come together in one flow, the harmony that is achieved allows the change to move through us upon its gliding, bubbling, laughing stream, a clear current, directed and without obstruction. Congruent on every level, our body hums with one intention.

To integrate and confirm, the action must be seen

While that intention may be clear and, through congruence, we may feel ourselves alive with the energy of potential and new growth, in order for it to slide into manifestation we must find the power of integration.

All rituals are shared and witnessed in some way, be it only by the birds and the bees, the trees and the ancestors, or, where there is a priest, a gathering of friends and family, community. The acknowledgement of the change by those who attend the ritual is a crucial step in securing that it is done.

The language we use for this is one of respect and honour, acknowledging the world around us not only as spirit but also as the beauty of creation. Communication is real, solid, grounded. Making offerings of our own creativity, the expression of the *awen* that we have tasted, we share it with those who have witnessed our change, knowing that the intention is played through and concluded.

RITUAL LANGUAGE

must accordingly have within it a clear intent which speaks to spirit, a flow of energy that engages with our subconscious perception, and an action that communicates to the outside world what has been done. Our intention, through congruence, slides into the creativity of manifestation.

WORDS AND PRAYERS

If we begin by understanding that no words are necessary, it is possible to relieve some of the anxiety about getting them 'right'. Having said that, words can be a potent aid.

First of all, the intention being the crucial part of any ritual, using words can help clarify that intention, not only to ourselves but also to those who witness and share the rite, those in body and in spirit whose presence influences the energy and focus of the experience. The intention of a ritual is very often declared aloud close to the beginning, the purpose and hopes being stated clearly to all who have gathered, both seen and unseen.

It is important to know to whom it is we are speaking. That may be obvious, a clear part of the intention, say, in a ritual performed to give thanks to an ancestor for his teachings, to the spirits of the land for the harvest, to the mother goddess for the birth of a child. Sometimes it isn't so clear. We may be calling for inspiration, for guidance, for clearer understanding, bathing in the beauty of an event, unaware of the source of such *awen*.

If we are not working with a specific deity, in the Druid tradition it is the spirits of place and the spirits of our ancestors that we speak to in our rituals. Often it is harder to perceive the ancestors, yet also it can be difficult to 'see' or 'hear' the spirits of a place. The key is not to try. So often our perception is muddied or blocked by an attempt to be 'psychic', when it is our normal human senses that will give us what we need. What is the strongest force of life in the environment close around us? The big tree by the stream perhaps, the sky above, the hill itself, the sea, the heather. It need not be the most powerful being, but it will be the one that is most clearly touching our awareness. It may be a dozen spirits, or the guardian of the whole valley or glade. It may be that we don't even see the spirit's creative manifestation, yet can feel its energy. It may be that we are simply asking these spirits to witness a ritual and our intention is focused more specifically upon a personal guide or teacher, in body or spirit. Whoever it is, within the intention of a ritual should be woven an understanding of to whom it is spoken.

It is so very important for effective ritual that the energy of our soul truth and spirit creativity flows freely through us, whatever words we use. If we naturally find ourselves poetic, then these words can be potent invocations. If no poetry slips easily from the tongue then it is better to use the words of daily living than to struggle and stammer, tripping up on an unfamiliar language. The words spoken must be meant.

In the same way, using other people's words, whether learnt by heart or read from a script, can allow us to make the sounds without spirit flowing through them. Another's text may give us teaching, may give us the confidence of using something that is apparently tried and tested, but we must understand and fully participate in each and every word, claiming them as our own truth, or they will be meaningless.

Working from a ritual that is wholly scripted not only denies us the opportunity to involve ourselves fully, even if the words are our own, but without the freedom of spontaneity we also lose the power of the relationship, of the moment, of presence. If a whole group is following the script it can hold attention and focus, particularly if many in the group are unfamiliar with the form, but in order to retain the power of the ritual, the sacred relationship simply cannot be tied to a script. Prayers and invocations, ideas and outlines can be written as guides, but no more, or the ritual risks becoming a piece of theatre *(see Drama below)*.

Some prayers have a power about them – old words used many times, words that have been consecrated and filled with the collective spirit of many priests and seekers in many rites over many years. Some of these are so inspired, carrying with them an unsaid invocation of the ancestors, that it is barely necessary to understand the individual words. Indeed, just as in Catholicism mass was said in Latin for so many centuries, in the Druid tradition the languages of Welsh, Old English and Gaelic are sometimes used for invocations and prayers, even when the words are not fully understand. Needless to say, there is a risk in this for those who don't speak the languages (for no words can ever be simply, fully and accurately translated), but if carefully chosen the prayers can be powerful in their inherent invocation.

Some of the old Druid prayers still used today come from the hand of Iolo Morgannwg, a Welsh stonemason of the eighteenth century who spent a good deal of his life studying and translating all he could find of old Druidry. Where he found gaps, he forged manuscripts, writing some of the best 'medieval' Welsh poetry himself. From his collection comes the 'Universal Druid Prayer'. This exists in many forms, both Morgannwg's own and versions adapted by modern Druids. One that is commonly shared is as follows:

Grant, O Spirit, thy Protection
And in Protection, Strength
And in Strength, Understanding
And in Understanding, Knowledge
And in Knowledge, the Knowledge of Justice
And in the Knowledge of Justice, the Love of it
And in the Love of it, the Love of all Existences
And in that Love, the Love of Spirit and All Creation.
(IM/BDO)

Words can be magical. They hold within them a thousand associations, each of which is able to evoke emotion, to invoke the spirits of a place, the ancestors of a time now past. Taking us out of the constraint of a difficult situation, words can be freeing, offering us the imagery of a changed, healed reality. Used in ritual, they are most potent when all their many associations are used consciously, carefully and respectfully, for their energy can flow with and change the course of the sub-conscious mind.

Words can also be doorways to the worlds beyond the mind, worlds seldom perceived by any but those who know they exist, the worlds of the faerie and other older races who have long lived amongst us at the edges of our knowing.

 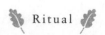

Stories take us upon journeys through worlds that our everyday perception finds it harder to accept. Exploring times and cultures that have long moved behind us, childhood mentalities we have now grown out of, stories keep our minds open to possibilities and realities that we don't live in day to day. Testing our imagination, honing our skills of creative visioning, stories keep open the doorways to strange worlds where we find teachings and inspiration that offer us the power of our potential. Stories tell of love and passion, beauty, grief and courage, leading us forward into richer lives.

Teaching us more deeply of the nature of spirit, stories within ritual guide us to move closer, to trust more fully the essence of life, its infinite resources of *awen* and its potent invulnerability. Teaching us of particular spirits of place, of ancestors and deities, stories of others' adventures inspire us to let go of more of our fears and inhibitions, dedicating ourselves to living in a sacred manner.

Tales of our ancestors, of connection with the land, of natural philosophy and natural lore, help release our sense of isolation, guiding us to understand where we stand in time and space, walking in the line of our ancestry, from distant grandparents to our descendants, and where our feet touch upon the sacred land. This process of self-location is an enormous part of the soul's quest for identity and a sense of soul belonging, and hearing, learning and sharing stories can be an effective part of that.

The tradition of accompanying a story with a harp is one which stretches back into prehistory. Some images of musicians playing the crotta, cruith or harp are over 2,500 years old and many Bards of the tradition still play as they tell their tales.

Though stories are often told within ritual, an important part of modern Druidry is the *eisteddfod*, another Welsh word meaning a 'sitting' or 'session', where the Bards, musicians, poets, balladeers and storytellers offer their creativity to the gathering around them. Though often this is done after the ritual has concluded, usually at the feast shared in celebration, on a fine day when the rites stretch through the afternoon or into the night, the *eisteddfod* may take place within the consecrated space, the stories being offered as gifts to the sources of inspiration. It is a time not only for the accomplished, but also for those beginning their training or study of the Bardic crafts, the sitting offering them a supportive forum in which to practise their creative expression, releasing shyness and inhibitions.

With metre added to the music of the voice, giving it a rhythm that serves to emphasize the imagery and emotion, a story slips into the form of a poem. It's a powerful medium, for when we listen to a great poem that truly inspires, we create instantly the weave of pictures and feelings, holding them not separate from our own lives but within ourselves and our own reality. Poems emerge from the soul, whether we listen to them or create them.

Connecting the spatial right and the linear left sides of the brain, balancing mental awareness, poetry brings pictures into words while still leaving spaces in between. It's these gaps which force the mind blindly to jump that prove so powerful in ritual situations, inspiring us to think somewhere off the trackways of expectation. Poetry leaves us unexpectedly open to new realities, watching the devas dance beneath the leaves, the energy of love shining blood red and gold, the blackbird chatting quietly to the apple tree, our own soul flying and diving through currents of life.

Much of the old British literature about our heritage and tradition is held in the form of poetry, and learning the craft of writing it is one of the key areas of study within the Druid tradition to this day.

Some of the greatest poems from the medieval literature are often used as prayers and invocations in ritual, including the one which follows, which is one of the best known. Spoken by Amergin, a mythical but probably once living Druid of Ireland, it is found with his story in the twelfth-century *Book of Leinster* and others. It speaks to us of our connection with the spirits of creation and the power imbued by such a vision of life:

I am the wind which breathes upon the sea,
I am the wave upon the ocean,
I am the murmur of the billows,
I am an ox of seven fights,
I am an eagle upon a rock,

I am a ray of the sun,
I am the fairest of all plants,
I am a wild boar in valour,
I am a salmon in the water,
I am a lake upon a plain,
I am a word of cunning art,
I am the point of a spear in battle,
I am the god who puts fire in the head,
Who brings light to the gathering on the hilltop?
Who announces the ages of the moon?
Who knows the place where the sun has its rest?
Who finds springs of clear water?
Who calls the fish from the ocean's deep?
Who causes them to come to shore?
Who changes the shape of headland and hill?
A Bard whom seafarers call upon to prophesy.
Spears shall be wielded,
I prophesy victory,
And all other good things,
And so ends my song.
(BL/PS)

Any poetry can be appropriate for use in a ritual. It is more important to attune it with the intention of the rite than to keep to any style, era or culture. Modern poetry can be as powerful as the old pieces. Some poetry is used to guide the mind into beauty, while other works are used to wake us into thinking. Because poetry does affect us deeply, it must be remembered that the effect of a poem can last for quite a while.

Both stories and poems are often used as a part of ritual even when the ritual is performed alone, witnessed only by the trees and the wind in their leaves, the shining moon and glinting stars, the spirit source of inspiration the rite is spoken to. As a part of our creativity, our own stories and poetry are given as sacred offerings of thanks, respect and exchange.

DRAMA AND MYTHOLOGY

Drama, on the other hand, is seldom (and not easily) performed alone, but can be the creative offering of groups, which, through sharing the laughter and tears evoked by the play, find their own bonds of community and understanding strengthened. For those that enjoy it, drama is an important part of shared ritual.

There is power in theatre, in reciting the lines of a play or ritual, particularly one that has been enacted many times before, its very recitation becoming an invocation of ancestral spirits. However, drama in Druid ritual is usually enacted without a script being written, read or recited. The players know the tale inside out and live its emotion through their own words and actions, evoking the passion and empathy in the circle of those gathered to watch, drawing them in to feel for themselves. The more interactive it is, the more powerful it can be, as everybody becomes involved, entangled in the plot's twists and turns, searching for the release of the ending.

Many of the stories played out are those of mythology, old tales of folklore, some of which are found in earlier versions in our medieval literature. Many of those are retellings of still older legends of the heroes and gods of these islands and the lands of our ancestors. Ritually dramatizing these stories brings them back to life, retaining them as an important resource of our heritage. If the players are skilled ritualists and the moment is appropriate, they may be acting as channels for the ancient spirits to move through; others, not used to such techniques, reach for the spirits' energy and inspiration while themselves consciously working into the roles. Obviously, where the energy is channelled, it is a more powerful performance, but the old spirits are not always amenable and a ritual play can tear off on a wild tangent ...

The power of myth is in its symbolism, for the stories are those replayed in nature all the time. Mythic tales explore the paradoxes and conflicts of life, of light and dark, love and grief, of lust and repulsion, good and evil, the wild and the tamed, the aspiring and decaying. So within the stories are teachings of nature, both that of humanity and of the worlds within which we live. With the language of drama being that of movement, emotion and imagery, it is a natural medium for congruence with our subconscious minds, exploring, affirming and encouraging change.

In modern Druidry, the rituals that mark the festivals of the year have within them perfect opportunities to play out mythic tales, those expressing the changing tides from the dark heart of winter through the birthing of spring to the slaying of the harvest and the frost-cleansing of the land. They offer potential for healing the wounds and taboos about decay and death, fertility and sexuality, stasis and change. There are many different mythic representations of this seasonal cycle which Druid Groves express in their own ways.

MUSIC AND DANCE

Music and dance are wonderfully effective elements of ritual for those who understand the language and can free themselves into it. Without the constraint of words that hold us too closely into specifics, the language of music and dance is simply that of the body, of energy and vibration. It allows us to express ourselves through melody, tone, gesture and movement, free from the risks of miscommunication that are possible within a verbal language that might not be wholly shared, where potent layers of associations may not be held in common. With music and dance, we don't try to understand; we simply feel.

Leaving the imagination to drift, gliding through pictures, memories, fantasies and abstract sensation, through music and dance we release our consciousness from the linear binds of its thinking-talking state and let go into the tides of rhythm and flow. Gliding on air currents, the warm thermals beneath our wings, floating on the open seas, held by the surge of sun-splashed waves, stamping and tiptoeing upon the grass, reaching up into the skies with the trees, the energy of natural *awen* pours through us.

Music and dance can lift us, pulling the spirals of our energy up, empowering, fuelling, setting us on fire, or can soothe and settle, guiding us back into the balanced calm of our sacred centre. Expressing our soul's creativity, we can offer our songs and movement as gifts to the sources of our inspiration, dancing for the gods, singing to the forest.

Traditional music, the folk music and dance of Gaelic cultures, of old English and Welsh, is often played in Druidry. Harps, lyres, flutes and tin whistles are seen to be more traditionally acceptable than guitars and cellos, yet in reality the oral tradition of spiritual creativity is more than happy to welcome music on any instrument, just as long as it is played with respect. So a piece for the *eisteddfod* of a ritual, or the sacred offerings of any individual, might come in the form of a traditional song or tune played upon a yew harp, or it may be a wild fusion of Gaelic and Arabic on hammered dulcimer, or the journey of one voice exploring the paths of some deep emotion. It is so much more important, in this medium as in any other, that the offerings are an honest expression of the soul, a flowing of spirit, of rich and blessed *awen*, than that they conform to any style or particular culture. Listening to the earth, to the wind in the trees, to the birdsong and the rhythms of passion, love and fear, we find our music and we share it, with honour.

Drums are a familiar instrument of ritual. The Irish bodhran is most commonly found, but also African djembes, Native American Plains drums and almost any other kind of percussion that will resonate with the earth.

Dance in ritual is sometimes to traditional steps, but more often than not it comes in the free style of personal expression as the individual is moved by the immediacy of power. Sometimes drums are played, while at other times it is the rhythm of the Earth that beats within us, urging us to move forward and into step with her, urging us to listen and to respond.

In ritual, dance can be the expression of our connection with nature. We dance the movement of the trees, the surge of waves. We might dance the form of animals we feel within our souls, or those in spirit that we know to be guiding us, and in doing so we strengthen our connection with these spirits, deepening our ability to empathize, to see the world through another's vision and so to learn. In this way our understanding of sacred creation grows.

The hardest part of dancing is often the breaking through of inhibition. Listening to music alone, allowing it to seep into our body until the vibration is filling us, we learn how to dance by stopping our thinking processes, simply feeling the energy and letting our body respond, allowing us to express the emotion and rhythm without the split-second delays of anticipating a move and the awkward hesitation of self-consciousness.

Releasing our physicality into the music of the harp, the drum or the wind, we learn the art of surrender into the flow of life's energy.

TRANCE, CHANTS AND MEDITATION

There are various reasons for trance in ritual. On a simple level, trance is one step deeper in the process of releasing ourselves from our thinking-talking consciousness into the *awen*. When we have set an intent and then let go of our thinking mentality, we are able to journey into the subconscious mind and the worlds that lie beyond our consciousness, free from the constraints of linear and logical perception. Trance allows us to move through shifting states of awareness, where illusion is stronger than solid reality, and therefore the potential for change is all the greater.

From the first steps beyond full consciousness to a place far outside the world of shared reality, trance is a spectrum of personal control. Losing ourselves into the rhythm of music or the beat of the drums, into the passion of love, we wander into the fringe of trance.

Reaching states of deep trance is not something we can learn to do overnight; while some people naturally, or as a result of some traumatic experience, can take themselves to this place which lies on the edge of madness, most need the guidance of a sound and well-reputed teacher to take them there and, more importantly, bring them back. Surrendering to such a teacher, one who is utterly trustworthy, is a powerful experience and not one to take lightly.

The now often-used technique of guided visualization is a first, easy and usually trouble-free outing into this adventure. In such journeys we are taken to places which, to whatever extent we are able, we believe to exist, at least within the realms of the mind. Our bodies respond to the sensory input given us by our imagination, our subconscious beliefs revealing themselves to us as we make our way through beauty and difficulties, learning all the way. In deeper trance, there is no consciousness that the journey is within the imagination. Indeed, those who are able move through doorways to other worlds beyond the imagination, encountering realms of spirit usually well hidden behind the dense physicality of the manifest world.

The value of trance is that it allows us a deeper connection with spirit than is often possible when the conscious mind is still awake and aware of mundane reality, retaining control of our journeying. For those who have no teacher at their side, the value can be gained simply in the art of releasing oneself into music, dance, beauty, creativity: letting go.

Fasting, sleep and sensory deprivation are other ways of inducing trance. Drugs, of course, are another doorway to trance often used in native traditions and nature religions. In Druidry as it is practised in our modern culture, drugs are not condoned in any way. Instead there is an understanding that if we can't reach the state of release with the power of our own mind, we have no business getting there.

Connecting spirit to spirit with a plant or fungus, instead of ingesting its toxic physical form, we can relate and experience the power of its energy in the same way that we find ecstasy and learning in any relationship, and the more so where there is surrender and love. The power of herbal remedies can be accessed in the same way, spirit to spirit, with respect.

Both meditation and chanting are often used in Druid ritual. Used for extreme periods they too can lead to trance states, but in the vast majority of rituals they are used simply as a tool for focus and concentration.

Meditation in Druidry is not a practice which aims at transcending the physical state. Simply by taking our attention into listening and seeing the spirit essence, concentrating more fully, we move into meditation, deep concentration. Rather than struggling to think of nothing, we are able more carefully to feel the flow of energy that is our own spirit connecting with the spirit of the land beneath our feet, the spirit of the tree beneath whose canopy we sit, the spirit of the ocean that whispers its song to us. In focusing on the beauty of that sacred interaction, our soul is refuelled, our questions are answered.

Many chants used in Druidry are created out of prayers or invocations, the words taken from the moment for the moment and its needs. The most commonly used chant in the Druid tradition is simply the word *awen*. As a chant it is pronounced *aaah–ooooo–ennnn*. Often it is chanted just three times, on one note, as an invocation of the spirit that is the inspirer. Sometimes, however, the chant is extended, its harmonies allowed naturally to rise and fall with the flow of energy. When many voices are weaving and cascading around and through each other, it is a powerful experience.

Another well-used chant is that of three key trees of the old Ogham alphabet. Ogham is a system of language, writing and mnemonics first recorded in Ireland in the second century CE, in which each of the 20 or 25 letters corresponds to a tree. The chant is in the Gaelic for silver birch, yew and oak: *beith–ioho–duir*. Silver birch is the tree that signifies birth, new beginnings and the cleansing processes of renewal. Yew is the tree of death and the magical knowledge of decay. Duir, the oak, is the tree of strength, stability and endurance. Some think of these three trees as symbolic of the three facets of the tradition, the crafts of the Bard, the Ovate and the Druid.

It is common for Druids to take trees that they work with, or are significant in the particular ritual they are doing, and use their names (in Gaelic, Welsh or English) as a chant. In doing so they focus their minds on the power of the trees while also using the associated mnemonics of the Ogham system.

THE LANGUAGE OF RITUAL

is the personal expression of our relationship with the sacred. In its honesty and soul truth, it is a language alive with the vibrant flow of *awen*. It is a language rich with the creativity of learning.

While this chapter has spoken of the different ways we can express ourselves in ritual, in the last section of this book, when we explore the rituals themselves, techniques will be given for understanding and experiencing these more fully.

In the meantime, we move on to look at where rituals are best performed: powerful, favourable and fashionable locations ...

the
SETTING

THREE LOCATIONS

The rain is falling, so finely that though I lift my face to the skies I can barely feel it on my skin. It lingers as mist in the fields around us, cloud that has drifted, silent, to the ground. Ahead of us the stones seem veiled in its quiet.

Stepping from the path and onto the damp grass, I can feel the shift in my heart and my fingers clasp more tightly the hand of my priest. He smiles at me, laughing inside at the excitement he sees filling my eyes. It's always the same.

We walk to the path of that perfect alignment, where the sun rises at Midsummer touching the Heel Stone on its way to the altar, and bowing to the spirits we too move towards the circle, our breath white in the cold dawn air as we call for acceptance before slipping through the sarcen trilithons and into the temple.

So aware of every movement of energy upon my skin, I walk the circle again and again, listening to the hum of the stones in my veins, feeling the way that it draws me in. And, again and again, I stumble through walls of air, each one taking me through some unseen shift in time, and voices murmur and quiver, drifting around me, spirits, men standing in a huddle of long capes, a horse rearing, its rider calling, an ethereal urgency, a ceremony of long ago, cloaks of feathers, each image unconnected, simply moving past me, a woman lying dying, empty, aching, cold. Through the stones I see the silhouette of a man standing still. He rubs his gloved hands together; a security guard of my own time. He smiles and turns away. I close my eyes and, for a moment, I am weightless, immovable, until the words of my intent slide again through my mind and again I walk on, asking for guidance.

When we come together, in the centre by the altar stone, I have lost my awareness of anything beyond. My priest gazes, wondering, touches my face and we look up. The veil of cloud has split above us, the deep blue of early morning seeping through. A crow, sitting high on a standing sarcen, caws quietly, listening to our tender laughter.

I throw my watch onto the pile of clothes strewn across the chair. Twenty minutes, I have 20 minutes. Glancing around me, appalled, I wonder what on Earth I can do. Stacking books and papers together into one heap on the bed, for a moment I spin, swirling, throwing shoes into the closet, before I sigh and give up. It's life. My life. Not a mess, but entirely lived in, the paraphernalia of my world scattered about me with easy abandon. A smile sneaks across my face. I shrug and lift the fat green candle from the bedside table.

Sitting down on the floor, setting it before me, I breathe deeply, my mind moving over the importance of this and that, framing the reason for the rite I'm about to do. 'Twenty minutes,' I whisper. More like 15; this needs to be simple. I lift the matches, striking one as I reach inside myself, clarifying, formulating, finding my direction. Lighting the candle, I hold my intent as if in the palm of my open hand.

'Hail, sweet spirit of the land beneath me, guardians of this hearth, spirits of this place ...'

But chuckles are rising from deep inside me. From somewhere there has crept out into the open landscape of my mind's eye a memory, that of my son as a young child softly calling to the purple monster he swore blind lived beneath his bed. I shake my head, laughing, knowing as I do so that this is the music of my rite being done.

The fire spits. There must be pine in the kindling. The smoke wafts towards me and I close my eyes, whispering inside, *'Take it up, wind-kin, take it up, through the trees.'*

As the breeze shifts, swaying, playing with the fire, I look up at the stars glinting in a dark sky, my focus gently returning to the rite that moves around me, some mythic tale being told by a laughing young Bard. His long green coat dances wildly about him as his hands play, emphasizing, captivating, and some 20 or more souls watch him, eagerly, intently, with smiles and surprise, rapt with their anticipation, though I'd imagine almost all of them have heard the tale before.

Tonight, instead of listening, I feel my soul stretching, wandering, my attention again drifting to the beauty of this place – a glade in the forest, a temple of old oak and beech, its spirit energy moving, pulsing, breathing an internal light, a circle of night sky roughly cut from the canopy, the edges of leafy branches shimmering above us in the breeze. Even with the Bard's words and the crackling of the fire, there is a sense of silence; it lingers around us like a presence, watching, holding us with its warm acceptance.

Three very real and very different ritual locations.

Stonehenge, a circle so much in the public eye, built by a political élite, standing in the midst of land now used by the military, is a place that is captivating. In some respects it exists as an archetypal sacred site, declaring its heritage as forcefully as it hides itself in veils of ancient mystery, provocative, extraordinary. The unique nature of its energy seems still to evoke an antagonism in any who feel themselves to be disenfranchized, dismissed by an 'authority' in power; perhaps that has always been the case.

The forest grove is a common place for Druids to gather, where public or private land allows. Indeed, it is traditionally thought that Druids' temples were groves of oak, this being yet another image given us by the Classical writers. Some, however, now believe that it was the Roman invasion that sent the Druids of the time into the cover of the forest. Certainly trees have always been considered deeply sacred in the tradition. *Bilé*, living sacred trees and carved wooden poles, were used throughout the islands as symbols of the tribal soul and strength. Circles and ovals of wooden posts, some roofed, were both forerunners to the stone circles and still being erected when the Roman occupation began halfway through the first century CE. Many of these were burnt or destroyed at the time of the invasion, to be rebuilt again, or built in the Roman style. There is no doubt that wooden temples as well as those of living wood were created and used for rituals.

As to the picture of the messy bedroom in a hectic life, I included it to show that a place appropriate for ritual need not be a circle built of stone and steeped in the energy of ancestral history. It need not be a place richly inspirited with the beauty of the natural world, with the energy of the wilderness little touched by humankind. Druid rituals can be performed anywhere.

THE REALITY OF ANYWHERE

Old stone circles and burial places are infused with an energy of our ancestors. Those who perform rituals in the forest, on the moors, in the meadows of our land, are searching for a different tone of energy to imbue their rites. Some seek out the old wells and natural springs, or create their temples upon the sand or shingle of the islands' shores. Some use the enclosed energy of the valleys while others reach up to the open skies from flat lands and hilltops.

Yet there are many within the tradition for whom the beauty of the countryside is an eerie and unfamiliar power, or where a sense of personal safety is only found closer to home. Temples are created in back gardens and indoors, in city parks and offices, some temporarily and others more permanently, altars holding a focus to a location that otherwise might be too chaotic with life's distractions.

The fact that we often find a need to perform a ritual where we perceive there to be no sacred space around us is an expression of what we understand to be sacred. Stuck on the verge of the motorway with a tired child and a suspiciously smoking car, swaying stupefied by the coffee machine when the boss has hurled files and abuse at your desk, unsure whether to laugh or cry as the computer simply stops or the cash machine burps happily, having eaten your card – the anomalies of life don't always happen to us at times when it's convenient to whisper, 'Excuse me,' and disappear to the place where our soul feels held, loved, nourished and refreshed. Our lives require us to be able to find those moments everywhere and anywhere.

UNDERSTANDING SACRED SPACE

It is so much easier to perceive the spirit or spirits in a beautiful environment, in the stones or cliffs, the trees and plants, the noise of the water tumbling over the rocks, the grass and the rising songs of the skylarks, the moonlight and the warmth of the hearth fire. Here we are able to feel our own spirit responding to the world around us, its strength and its beauty reflecting onto our own. These places are sacred to us; they are our natural temples. In Druidry, a temple is simply a place where we know we are nourished on a level that is soul deep.

Many of us know where these places are for us yet we simply don't have the time, resources or discipline to get there as often as we could, would or should. If these obstacles are surmountable, the first step in our practice of honouring ourselves, and the life force that flows through us, is to dedicate ourselves to making time, spending resources, getting to our temples. Once we are there, allowing ourselves to be deeply nourished by the sacred nature of the place, we can respond, with thanksgivings of our creativity, so deepening our relationship with the spirits that reside there.

To see the essence of life can be horrendously difficult when the energy and matter of creation seem to be attacking our very ability to survive it. Yet in acknowledging the spirit within life we are able to feel the strength of the sacred, its invulnerability and freedom, and so feel sufficiently safe to open and receive the energy of life, the pure creative force.

The word *nemeton*, an old British word which was thought to mean 'a grove', is now understood to translate more accurately as 'a sacred sanctuary'. Where we see the spirit of the natural world around us, we find our sacred sanctuaries. When, soul-naked yet free, we feel our own spirit touched, we know we have reached our *nemeton*. These are the temples of the Druids.

Sometimes it feels just too hard to find beauty and calm in a crazy world of violence and pollution, yet without being able to do so our vision can only add to the devastation, affirming its existence and its power over us. So the Druid will reach into matter to touch the spirit, to share strength and find inspiration, so beginning the process of positive change. Yet at times where it is desperate, in order to grasp our own ability to see the creative source, we must find some measure of our own strength first. So it is that, although in the tradition many temples are made where the spirit is singing its rich exuberance around us, it is through working on our own vision of the sacred that Druid temples are created.

The technique is simple but takes some practice. Before long it becomes a tool we can use in the most fraught of situations, but in learning how to do it we begin by finding a quiet place where we will not be disturbed.

Stand comfortably, feet apart, hips directly above your feet, your shoulders above your hips, so that your body can sway without losing balance. Check the weight of your head is balanced on your shoulders so as to give the neck as little stress as possible. Loosen your arms by gently shaking them free of tension. Be aware of any tightness that remains in your fingers and shake it out. In your face, the muscles of the jaw and around the eyes may need to be stretched with a wild wide yawn before you can find relaxation.

Fully feel the physical contact of your feet upon the ground. Then allow yourself to be aware of the energy of the earth, the pull that holds you, supports you, feeds you. You may feel this as a spirit light or a brilliant darkness, a pool of energy around your feet. Be aware of how you naturally breathe it in, drawing it up through your body like a tree drinking in the mineral-rich water of the soil, like sap rising through the branches that reach into the skies. Feel the air upon your skin, your face, the skies above, the light of the sun that inspires us to stretch and grow, the warmth of its power pouring down through your body. Be conscious of the balance that is the flow of the energy, both earth and sky, weaving through your body with the natural ease that is life. This is not something you are invoking; you are simply becoming aware of what is always happening.

Centred in this way, conscious of the most powerful forces, above and below, become aware of your own body of energy. The focus for sacred ceremony is that part we call the intimate space; this is the area immediately around us that we protect from intrusion by anyone except those with whom we have an intimate relationship. We flinch, tightening our intimate space, if we feel it is threatened. It is within this space that the deepest wounds are inflicted by life. It is within this space that we grow in the world, expressing our soul truths. When this part of us is flinched and scarred, we fail to grow. It is here that we make the important changes.

Our intimate space is our personal portable sanctuary in the world. When we are happy and calm and with those we love, we extend that energy body, relaxed, free. It is this ability to extend our intimate space that we learn when we create sacred space.

So, centred, become aware of your intimate space. Where is it relaxed and where is it flinched? Check behind and below, above and all around you. Then stretch it out. Create a circle, an even sphere with you at the centre. Make sure you are expressing your true self by pouring the energy of your naked truths into this space.

Knowing that the boundaries are strong, allow yourself to feel what would be your vulnerability within this space. Flex the muscle you used to stretch it out and change its shape. Withdraw it to its normal distance from your physical body. Some find it easier to extend and some to pull it in.

Don't expect to do it perfectly the first time. There are many reasons why it can be hard. If the boundaries don't feel secure, it is the practice of ritual with its invocations of guides and spirits that enables us to seal those edges so that we can feel entirely strong. It is through ritual, too, that we learn to feel the power of our own spirit invulnerability, the essence of our own life force that is the silent still-ness at the centre of the swirling of our lives.

If at any time you lose your sense of balance, return through the process of centring once again. When ready to return to normal consciousness, simply pull your intimate space back to what is naturally comfortable in your environment. If being conscious of the flow of earth and sky energy through you has made you dizzy, make sure that the energy *is* flowing, not getting stuck. Its flow should ground you naturally, drawing you down to touch the earth while freeing your living movement.

This is the way every ritual can begin and end, with this simple practice of perceiving the world's energy flowing around and through you.

Once we feel confident that we can use this intimate space as a conscious tool, we can stand within it and look at the world around us. What is flowing through us? What is consistently pushing against us? What are we fighting? What simply ignores the bounds of our intimate space? The energy of children, the trees, cats ...?

This intimate space, the sacred sanctuary of our physical form, is the first and most important step to understand. Without a strong and familiar knowing of what is safe for us, we can fool ourselves into situations which do not feed us, or hold us in long-term stress. Knowing our intimate space is also an essential prerequisite to knowing what our ritual environment should feel like. If we are working a rite alone, this sense of intimate sanctuary should remain with us throughout the ritual. If we are performing the rite with others, being secure with our own understanding of sanctuary allows us to hold a powerful sense of spirit, as well as giving us a standard of what can be achieved in a cohesive group, a group where intimate space is shared.

THE INNER TEMPLE

Understanding that our intimate space is the sacred sanctuary of the physical body, the temple we carry with us around the flesh, blood and bones of our creative journey, we then turn in the tradition to find a sanctuary within our souls.

Survival of the body is closest to the instinctive drive of our animal nature, yet our human self-consciousness spins visions of threat out of the material world and into the psyche. There are demons of expectation and anticipation within us that only manifest in matter as reflections and projections.

Finding a full sense of sacred sanctuary, then, must also include a sense of perfect safety and nourishment within the self. This is done by the creation or discovery of a *nemeton* within our soul, a place within the mind that is wrapped and held by the intention of it being a sanctuary.

What is this place? For some it is a grove of trees, while others find for themselves a cove by the sea. It can be absolutely anywhere that is inspirited and perceived to be sacred, secluded and entirely safe. It is a special place, a place of our own, somewhere that cannot be touched by others, or by our own self-negation.

The more often we visit this inner temple, the stronger this place becomes. As a journey of the mind, it pushes us to develop our imagination and its value to us increases the more effectively we can experience it. Usually beginning visually, we explore it using our ability to hear the wind and the birdsong, to smell the earth, the stones, to feel beneath our fingertips the roughness of the bark. Using all our senses allows us to use the sanctuary as a place that evokes our emotions, reaching our subconscious paradigms, giving us the opportunity to express anger, grief, fear, desolation, in an internal environment which is wholly and naturally supportive. We can also feel the exhilaration of joy and ecstasy in such a place, strengthening our ability to reach the positive and creative.

Ritual in the tradition is sometimes simply a journey to this inner sanctuary to find an inner calm and sense of well-being. Often it is enough just to be there, to stretch out on the grass and watch the stars above the trees, to sit by the water and, eyes closed, let go into the sound of the surf.

When the inner sanctuary is secure and we are confident in our ability to reach it, to understand its language, it is possible to journey there and perform rituals that are more complex. Such rituals will have a clear impact on the self, touching spirit around us, but if they are to have an immediate effect on our outer world some physical act still needs to done. Yet if it isn't, the effects of inner change will gently seep out anyway.

As with so many aspects of Druid ritual and practice, the inner temple can also be a doorway to worlds beyond the imagination, a place where we encounter spirit as spirit, a place where spirit manifests its creativity in forms that it is hard to perceive through the mundane world. While adventuring in these 'otherworlds' of spirit can be dramatically more potent, in other ways the effect is the same: we develop our ability to see and hear in an environment where the wide skies of potential are that much richer and our responsibility for every step we take is vividly obvious.

Sometimes there is a fine line between our imagination and the worlds beyond. For some it is easy to reach the otherworlds, the natural barrier of doubt that slides in during childhood never having made much impression on their beliefs. Other people spend a great deal of time trying to break through. It can be easier to accept that the worlds beyond are still within the imagination, than reach a level of surrender that allows us to believe we have moved into another place.

Clear intent, responsibility and surrender are all powerful tools of exploration and change, and if these are being used well the metaphysics and neurological analysis of soul realities become a matter for interest and not validation. On some level we know if we are fooling ourselves or really making progress (even if only in retrospect).

THE CIRCLE CAST

One of my teachers told me clearly that any temple created by a priest should, at the end of the rite, leave no more trace on the environment than the energy humming in the air. He was not a lover of stone circles but a priest of the forest who could walk upon the ground and leave no footprint behind him.

The value and beauty of a momentary temple is profound. There is an exquisite feeling to knowing that, even after an amazingly transformative ritual experience, perhaps adorned with flowers, candles, incense, flowing robes and more, when the closing comes and everything is packed away, no sign is left of anyone having been there. There is the sense that it was an extraordinary dream and the entirety of the experience is carried away as our own.

Where there is no outer structure, be it a building or circle of stones, or even a circle of trees, the need to create the boundary of a ritual temple is more exacting. Not only does this hold the focus of attention, but it also contains the energy of the ritual in one place, allowing us to keep a sense of sanctuary, intimate space, even when there are no physical borders or walls.

In modern Druidry this is done by casting a circle. By walking the circumference, the edge of the temple space, we draw in the air and upon our minds the boundary line. We can use an outstretched finger, a wand of consecrated wood, a sacred dagger or any such thing (and each leaves a different impression according to our vision, our associated beliefs and expectations), but our intention is the most important part of the action.

It is possible to extract the temple space entirely from time and place, cutting the circle out of the web that connects it to the rest of reality, as if we had closed and barred the doors of a temple. Nothing done within the circle can affect the world outside it until the circle is opened, and at the same time nothing in the world outside can touch those within the temple, the energy remaining contained and detached.

In a family rite, however, or a ritual held in public, or with those attending who are not completely familiar with the form, binding a circle so tightly is not appropriate. The energy of those present must be allowed to flow more easily, with the world still to some extent influencing those in the ritual through its process. It is not expected that the poignancy of shared intimate space is reached or retained for long. In such a rite, the temple location is still scribed to hold the attention and energy focus in one place, but the circle is not detached; instead there is a weaving of souls together, an understanding of an intention shared. A temple like this may be marked out with music, with a scattering of flowers or seeds, or simply by holding hands.

CHOOSING A TEMPLE SPACE

If choice is available, intuition is the first tool to use when choosing a place to work a ritual. An open mind, without assumptions or expectations, will make a sounder decision than one constrained by hopes and premonitions.

It is usually best simply to be led by opportunity. Doors open before us and we step through, tasting the air, wondering, watching. Seeing the location in a vision, dreaming it is right, then searching it out can be a wonderful experience, but can be equally frustrating. Not all visions are prophecies; far more reveal potentialities and projections of hopes and fears. Clarifying our intent, as simply as possible, asking for inspiration and walking the steps gently will more likely take us to where the ritual will be appropriate, accepted and beautifully held.

Once a location has been found, the spirits of place should always be asked if it would be appropriate for the ritual to be performed within their energetic space. This is not a formality. The trees and the grass, the birds and beetles, the ancestral spirits and the faerie folk will all be affected by the energy of a ritual as much or more than they will influence the ritual's process. Of course, it would take some time to ask every creature, seen and unseen, for their permission, even if that were possible, but most places will have a governing spirit, a key feature in the local environment, such as a large oak, a line of rhododendrons, a burial site, some feature which obviously affects the energy and life flow of the area. Simply asking the guardian spirit of a place for its acceptance is usually enough.

The response must be certain. Even if the person who asks can't hear the voice of spirit, the energy will change. An approving smile brings a wash of clear and easy energy, allowing the ritual to begin without a hitch. A strong sense of the spirits moving away should always be accepted as a 'No' and the ritual should be relocated if it is to be done at all.

Doubt must be acknowledged. It may not mean that the spirits are unhappy but that some element of the rite is wrong, badly thought out, disrespectful. In my experience it is usually the case that doubt expresses a misplaced assumption. In other words, when the spirits are asked if a ritual can be done, they (together with our own subconscious) pick up on the whole intent and its potential, and when they question the validity of our expectations we feel the doubt. We might be assuming the cows in the field play no part, or the rain will stay away, or the baby will sleep, or ... Checking our intention and our expectations, then asking the guardian spirits again can clear the doubt. If it doesn't, it is usually best to relocate or reschedule. An unwanted ritual can be seriously detrimental, leaving traces of negative energy in the participants for a very long time, sometimes even years.

Some temples, such as forest groves, will thrive on the energy of ritual. A grove might adapt to the group which celebrates beneath its canopy, might be happy to accept its offerings, the music of its creativity and laughter, sharing the process utterly. Such a grove can become established, with well-trodden paths leading to it through the forest, the trees growing strong and proud with the attention.

Sometimes a glade will support a ritual group for a while, its spirits curious and willing to interact with the people, until the rituals performed there start to influence the glade's energy, altering the trackways (both physical or energetic). The group's presence has then become too much and is no longer welcome; it is time to move on.

If using a location outside, especially if that place is in an area of wilderness or seldom touched by humanity, it is important to be highly sensitive to the spirits of place and their changing tides.

Even an established temple needs to be asked whether it is appropriate for a ritual to take place. Asking the caretakers and/or landowners is an suitable first step, for they often (but not always) express the will of the spirits they protect, especially if they have lived and worked with the place intimately for some time. Then, when gathered on the day, with the ritual intention clear, the guardian spirits of the place should be asked as well.

It should not be assumed that any ancient stone circle or other old human-made temple will still be amenable to human contact. There are circles out on the moors, deep in the forests and valleys, high on the mountains, that are more populated now by the spirits of place, the wind and the rain and the prickly heather, the faerie and devas. Such old places have become unaccustomed to the noise and clumsy action of human beings and are more likely to play tricks than support sensitive rituals.

Where permission is offered, however, stone circles can be glorious places in which to perform ritual. Some circles in the Pretannic Isles have a history of religious practice dating back some 7,000 or 8,000 years, from the earliest archaeological traces of burial and sacrifice through wooden structures and standing stones, circles, offerings and later burials to the present day's reflections and extensions of traditions. When the history of one place is so strong for that long, it is possible to allow the mind to move further back still, thousands of years, imagining our ancestors reaching for their own connections with the powers and spirits of nature, searching for sanctuary, for peace and freedom from fear. At such places it is possible, too, to look forward into the future when our descendants will be making their offerings still.

Lone standing stones, carved stones, places that were obviously marked by our ancestors as particularly powerful places, used as altars for focus and for offerings to the gods and the dead, are also used by the Druids of today. Momentary rituals of thanksgivings and prayers, enriched with offerings, and more formal rites, using the stones as altars in the same way, have the same energy around them, the scent of the ancestors, teachers, watchers. At these places, the need to honour the spirits of place is paramount, for without it any connection is not only disrespectful to the place, but also to our ancestors and our heritage, to the land itself and the flow of life's *awen*.

But not all stone circles are ancient. Stone circles and altars are being built in gardens, both wild and suburban, across the land. Indeed, when I put my house on the market a few years ago, the agent told me that the stone circle was the main reason why the place was sold so quickly – in fact, it went within a day. My circle in that garden was nine foot across, made of stones dug from a derelict Somerset mine by a cave-diving friend who was clearing it for exploration. They were little more than 18 inches high, some sparkling with crystal, washed and shaped by centuries of underground water flows. It was an exquisite circle, with a fire pit in the middle around which we would sit late into the night.

There are some Druids who are now building much bigger circles, using 18 ton stones, which they erect very successfully using the neolithic technology of logs and hemp rope ... and sweet-talking the stone spirits. Such large circles can be created to align with solar and lunar tides, with surrounding sacred spaces and/or with the magnetic currents, so attuning the temple to the larger flows of the Earth's energy.

Druids are also planting groves of trees to be used as sacred sites, both on private land and in town parks and gardens in co-operation with local councils. Some groves are beautiful, with each variety of tree being carefully chosen for its magical and folkloric significance.

Creating sacred space that is built to last, in the form of stone circles, labyrinths and shrines, with wooden structures, trees and groves, allows us to view our spiritual journey within a wider picture. Temples built now will be there for our descendants, just as our ancestors have left us their sacred stones and altars, together with the wisdom that these places still contain. Perceiving the value of our lives and our responsibility for our legacy in terms of centuries or even millennia can only be healthy.

tools and
OFFERINGS

 WE have spoken of the venue. Now our focus turns to what we might wear, and with what accessories, and what we might take as a gift.

THE ESSENTIALS

There are none. If we can't make a ritual work with no tools whatsoever, we have no hope of making it work with a clutter of props. The foundation of Druid ritual is reverence for the natural world and celebration of its power and beauty; it is about our relationship spirit to spirit, about what we believe in and how that influences our relationship, spirit to spirit, and our ability to give and receive within it. If our hands are open and our hearts are open, our ears and eyes willing to understand, we have a better chance of connecting with the sources of our inspiration, with the powers of nature, than if our fingers are clasped around some implement, our minds skitting amongst the shiny cutlery on the altar.

Starting with an understanding that nothing is necessary, we can then begin to look at what might be inspiring, what might guide us to ensure that the three stages of ritual practice – communicating with spirit, with our own subconscious and with the world around us – are performed effectively and with abundant beauty and respect.

Tools, robes and equipment for ritual, then, should be used only as an expression of our rich creativity. The willing body, the focused mind and the vision of our spirit are really the only essentials for effective ritual.

ROBES

Though many begin their ritual practice without robes, there often comes a time when even the most reticent starts to dream of a length of material, the way it flows, its colour and texture in the sunshine or firelight. This is especially the case if we are working in a Grove of Druids, all or many of whom regularly don exquisitely beautiful robes, handcrafted from visions or discovered in little boutiques somewhere off the beaten track.

There is no uniform of colour in the tradition, though some Orders do work with certain ideas from various old manuscripts. White robes are very often used, symbolizing the highest light or attainment of knowledge, while many robes are of naturally undyed and unbleached fibre, giving the impression of an off-white robe. Some Druids consider the potency and vibration of colour more important, wearing the blues of the ocean, greens of the forest, of leaves and meadows, greys of thunderclouds, red of the bloodlines, browns of earth, black of night and the womb of creation.

Yet why wear a robe at all? One reason is that when we step into ritual clothes, we step into the mindset of perceiving the sacred world. It is one of a number of ways in which we move from mundane perception to the state of mind needed in a ritual. Other ways include:

- Ensuring there will be no distractions, taking the telephone off the hook, leaving clear 'Do Not Disturb' signs, giving ourselves a sacred period of seclusion.
- Bathing, perhaps in water scented with essential oils or an infusion of aromatic herbs or flower petals.
- Changing the lighting, closing the curtains, turning off electric lights, using only candles, lanterns or firelight.
- Changing into clothes and jewellery that are used only for ritual or special and sacred occasions.

The preparations are exciting, our body hums with anticipation, we expect change, deep nourishment, strength, positive affirmation, a sense of our own beauty and autonomy. We may associate the robes with all that we are given through our connection with the community with which we celebrate, the community of our ancestors and the spirits of place. They are also a part of our gift to ourselves and to the spirits, the gods, our sources of inspiration.

Of course, when ritual is performed spontaneously, the need to change into special clothes is quite irrelevant, and it is healthy not to have developed a belief that *only* by getting into a certain costume can you create the necessary mental shift. Rather like a young baby who is used to sleeping only in its cot and nowhere else, there soon comes a time when the rigidity of that structure is utterly constraining. We must hold onto our adaptability, keeping supple the muscles of our flexibility. Our robes should be a part of our creativity, not a necessity.

THE ALTAR

The value and use of an altar is as an enduring tool for focus. When our sanctuary, both of our body as intimate space and the inner temple of our mind, is strong enough to be unaffected by distraction, our spirit centre is the pivot, the balancing point, with our consciousness taking our perspective wherever it will. When the world around us is buzzing with distraction, the focus point of an altar is quite invaluable.

There are too many to count, tiny and smooth, some ridged and some curving into themselves, their colours softened yet somehow still so very rich, gold and burgundy, ivory shells, sea blue and hazel brown, as if being so long in the water has allowed the pigment to be absorbed more deeply than sunshine could ever fade out, than the tumbling of waves upon the sand could wear out. The candlelight dances on the deep blue of the glass bowl, my eyes drawing me into the spirals of shells, the spirals of time. In the silence of the room and my memories, the tides of the ocean are rising within me.

There's gentle laughter, the sound of people not sure quite what to do yet charmed, hesitant, wondering with respect. I turn from the circle of guests, following the beaming eyes of the bride, to see a robin has landed upon the altar, a millstone perhaps 3 feet across. I whisper a welcome and he hops across the green

Ritual

silk cloth towards me, then up onto the rim of the carved wooden bowl. The scent of the incense must be intriguing him, for with his head on one side for a moment he watches it in the censer. Then, reaching down into the offering bowl, he tugs off a piece of soft fresh bread. He looks around him and we can almost see his smile as he holds the snowflake of bread in his little sharp beak. He flies away, leaving us floating in quiet sunshine.

The pale bone-grey of the bird skull in the leaves upon the altar log seems to light up with curiosity in the fire's light, flames reaching up as if questing, untethered, fuelled by the energy of spirit and illusion. The priestess moves her arms, clearing her vision, her elbows cleaving through the smoke that rises in her mind, playing with its quick sharp timidity, so responsive, shifting, it darts from her touch then lingers, drifting, weightless as if carefree. The raven's feathers in my fingers gently beat against the air, lifting our bodies, our temple upon the wind, high into the canopy, through the dark foaming cloud, out into the indigo dark of nowhere at all. And as we rise I feel what it is she holds, the claws gripping tightly around her feet, and when she laughs I feel it slipping loose, falling, falling into the fire. My eyes open, a moment's glance held by the bronze chalice in the leafmould, the last of the evening's sunlight touching it with gold.

There's nobody here. I breathe deeply and sigh, exhaling every last whisper of breath in my lungs. The water is cool as I wash my hands and I gaze at myself in the over-lit mirror, knowing that if I don't find my centred strength now I'm going to break down and cry; knowing too that such emotion would not help the situation. Pulling the silver chain from around my neck, I let the leaf fall into the cup of my hand. A real leaf, a tiny oak leaf dipped in silver, it glints at me now and all I am slides into the stream of my perceiving it, sensing the oak from which it came, the power of the tree's spirit glowing in my open hand, an altar to its strength, the cycles of its life, the cycles of mine.

The trunk has bent over with the ease of age and, as I step down into the gully once a pathway of the brook, I can sense its roots stretching down beneath me, washed by the current that still seeps through the earth, through rich dark mud flexing with life. Encouraged by the boughs that rest on the grass, I sink to my knees, my fingers running over the ridged grey bark. 'Hello, dragon,' I murmur, laying the roses at its base. The deep red of their petals lingers in my mind, sharp in the misty air of dawn, as I close my eyes to make my prayers.

An altar might be dedicated to one god or goddess, to a pantheon of gods, to one's own blood ancestry or the ancestors of the land that feeds us, or those who lived in the house or on the land before us. It may be dedicated to an elemental force, such as water and the seas, or earth and its fertility, its sweet fruitfulness. It may be placed beside or before an object that is revered – a mountain, spring or forest, the ocean or valley – and in this way act as an offering table to the spirits who hold that power.

What is needed on an altar is no more than whatever we ourselves wish to put on it. If the altar is a stone or tree, that in itself is enough. It may be a table in the corner of the room, an old slab of wood at the bottom of the garden. Altar cloths might be used, left *in situ* or brought for an occasion. On an altar to our ancestors, family photographs might be placed. Any artefact or object which expresses the beauty and power of the forces which we are honouring through our altar will guide us to focus better – seashells, pine cones, leaves, stones, fossils or pictures. The important point to remember is that the altar is an aid to focus, and the mental and emotional associations we have with everything we place upon it must be considered. An object that is distracting will not necessarily be useful.

Candles are perhaps one of the most helpful tools. Lighting a candle on an altar clarifies our focus, bringing us back to perceive the sacred, while at the same time being an act of thanksgiving, honouring whoever it is that the altar is revering.

POWER OBJECTS

Power suffuses an object from its spirit core and that spirit, together with the soul, heart and body, is strengthened by gifts of honour and appreciation. Anything that is loved and respected soon starts to glow with confidence, the spirit's invulnerability starting to shine through. In human beings, self-consciousness and inse-

curity mixed with gifts of devotion can create an untenable ego, but in the non-human world this is seldom the case, for energy naturally keeps flowing.

Power objects, or those objects which have been infused with appreciation, their spirits' nature and strength revered, are important elements of sacred ritual. Feathers from birds that are especially loved by the person performing the ritual, bones, horns, antlers or hide from an animal or species of animal that the person has a particularly strong connection and relationship with are all examples of important power objects used in the old traditions.

Crow feathers worn in the hair, a cloak crafted of deer skin, a badger's claw or fox tooth hung around the neck, an ox horn used for mead, an oyster shell or frog bone set upon the altar, all serve to bring the practitioner or priest a deeper focus. They act as a medium, too, for communication with the spirits of these creatures, enhancing relationships, allowing us to learn more closely the lessons of another creature, another soul's perception.

Nobody who uses these items as tools of power would come close to harming such a creature, and the objects are usually found in the wild, in roadkills or through a network within the community where such things are given as sacred gifts. Paying for them would be an act of dishonouring the spirit, with the risk of encouraging a trade that could endanger wildlife (though nature's laws of exchange are always required).

Needless to say, power objects need not come from animals. Pebbles and stones are equally used – those with exceptional markings, streaks that express distinct stories and times, hues and tinges of different mineral residues, beautiful shapes and colours smoothed by the sea, carved by the wind, roughened and chipped. The energy of the earth is held in these stones, evoking memories of our own lives and the lives of our ancestors way back into the mists of time. Again they are used as tools for focus, reminding us of the power beneath our feet.

While an animal spirit will carry the energy and wisdom of both its species and its own life, the ability of crystals to hold information other than their own stories is well known. They are potent tools for ritual, yet at the same time they are little understood. Crystals can hold intention and redirect energy in a way that can make changes beyond what we might perceive. They retain information, much of which may not be grasped by those who work with them, for their abilities and scope are too easily underestimated. If crystals are used in Druid ritual, they are treated with extreme caution and respect.

Many in Druidry, however, as in any other native/nature tradition, would rather work with a stone that was found in their own forest than one possibly blasted from the earth in a distant land. In this way, we are less likely to misunderstand its language and the wisdom it holds.

Plants, herbs and trees are often used as power objects, each species carrying the wisdom of its own natural lore, its unique understanding and connection with elemental power, with the land beneath us, with the cycles of time. While never coming close to the reality of its knowledge, through empathy and creating relationship spirit to spirit, working with a 'witness' such as a piece of wood, a leaf, seed or nut, we can start to touch upon the power of that being.

There are many fabulous books that document the folkloric associations and medicinal uses of plants, herbs and trees. While not dismissing these, the Druid tradition teaches us to go out and find the plant itself, explore its environment, understand it *in situ*, before using any part of it that has been harvested. This allows us a totally different and far more sensitive, mutually responsive attitude. We connect spirit to spirit and so understand the plant's potential and its *own* intention.

The same can be said with regard to the food we eat. With a sacred perception, our diet naturally changes as we learn how to value the life force, unblinkered.

Also, by carving a piece of wood or stone into the form of a tree, creature or elemental, we can effectively infuse it with power, the relevant spirit having been invoked by the carving. The same can be done by engraving markings or words in old sacred languages such as the Nordic/Germanic runes or Gaelic Ogham. While not the genuine animal or tree, the object can become a medium through which a relationship with that animal or tree can be strengthened. Using such an object will continuously reinforce the carving's ability to hold the spirit we are calling.

INCENSE

Incense is often used in Druid ritual, mostly to consecrate or cleanse a temple space or a power object. This is either done with dried herbs tied together into a thick bundle that can be lit or with a mixture of dried herbs, resins, petals, seeds and berries, oils and bark which make up a more complex incense to be burnt on a special charcoal block.

The choice of incense is entirely dependent on the ritual's intent, who is gathering for it and where it is to be held. Special mixtures can be bought or made up so that an incense is as appropriate as possible, honouring the spirits of place as well as all the spirits whose creative energy is in the incense mixture itself.

When charcoal blocks are used for burning incense mixes, censers are needed. These can be extremely ornate, of bronze or iron, so the pungent smoke coils out in swirling serpent dances. A simpler censer might be a chunk of flint or other stone.

FIRE

Fire is a wonderful tool for ritual. Offering us a central focus in a sacred circle, or an altar focus through the flames of a candle, it is often considered the element that is most powerfully transformative.

Frequently in ritual some way of making offerings to the ancestral spirits is required and fire is an ideal medium, for it takes the physical and reduces it to its pure spirit essence, where, spirit to spirit, it can be shared.

Where ritual requires a symbolic or actual process of release, again very often fire is the perfect channel. Representations of what we are letting go can be given into the ever-changing, bright-flickering, consuming flames.

A ritual fire might be made in the hearth at home, in the fire pit of an outside temple or in a cauldron or cast-iron fire dish. Special woods can be used, or a selection of wood, chosen with a consciousness of the trees' qualities and wisdom, according to natural lore, herbalism and personal relationship.

As long as the spirits of place are comfortable with a fire being lit, safety precautions are adhered to so that the environment is honoured and unharmed, and the fire spirits are content to behave in the best interests of all who are gathered together, fire is a very powerful tool.

THE BOWL

All kinds of bowls and cups are used in ritual. A bowl might receive offerings that are given to the gods, the ancestral spirits and others invoked and present; a cup or chalice may hold the water with which the temple space might be consecrated; another cup may hold the mead, wine, ale or other drink that is a meaningful part of ritual celebration.

While not always present physically, the cauldron is perceived by many as the most important 'bowl'. The Holy Grail may be seen as the refined version of the rough bronze or iron cauldron, the pot within which the gods of our ancestors brewed the essence of inspiration. Like the old cauldron, the Grail too holds the power of rebirth. To drink from it is to drink the fluid essence of *awen*, the milk of the gods, and legend tells us that in doing so we risk death, madness or glorious inspiration ...

Symbolic of the womb, the power of the feminine creative source, the black iron cauldron holds the terror of true potentiality, the depths of the unknown, the dark void of the universe, infinite and boundless. It expresses the law of nature within its form, yet at the same time it is formless, for the sides of the cauldron are but a part of its power: the space within is the body of its mystery.

Some feel it important to have specially blessed and beautiful cups to use in ritual. Yet the ornate silver chalice, the intricately carved and polished wooden offering bowl, the custom-made cast-iron cauldron are easily replaced by the teacup, the cereal bowl and the kitchen pot by those for whom their integrated value is just as important. Alternatively, there is certainly a poignant benefit in using a sacred offering bowl as a bowl to eat from or a consecrated cauldron to cook potatoes in, and the artificial divisions between the sacred and mundane are broken down in this way. Keeping some items specially for ritual is, however, also worthwhile, for simply bringing out these tools allows our subconscious minds to connect with the associated images of ritual and the sacred. We learn from both ways.

WEAPONS

From the symbolic feminine power held by the cauldron, we move to blades, knives, swords and wands. Each of these is used as a tool for directing the energy and flow of intention.

Here is the blade that shimmers with the symbolic power of masculine creativity; it is the penis that balances the energy of the womb, offering the pointed clarity of penetration, a straight beam of light entering the dark. The joining of the two forces offers a further symbolic representation of the power of germination, conception, creativity.

Yet, in the same way that the power of the cauldron is in the darkness it holds, so the mystery of the blade is in its *potential* severity. It can cut just as the bowl can carry, but there is teaching in the poignancy of leaving its razor-sharp edge untouched as well as in the actual use of the blade. In Druid ritual it seldom makes a scratch.

The sacred dagger has been refined through the evolution of myths and tales from the rough squat blade into the sheer elegance of Excalibur. This sword of sovereignty, that holds within it the power of dignity, honour, duty and valour, expresses the tempering of male energy in our culture in the same way that the cauldron became the Grail, women's energy for a while being held firm within the taming hands of a male-oriented society.

In the tradition today, all kinds of blades and cups are used, with associations of gender, power, beauty and force being perhaps more complex, unique and individually understood than ever before.

The wooden wand has a different value from the blade, though it is still a tool for directing energy. Often a Druid will find the necessary wood as a fallen branch, but when it is still living wood, he will talk to the tree spirits, honouring the flow of life, asking for the length of wood, clearly expressing his intention to use it in a sacred manner. If the tree agrees, the wood can be cut cleanly and sensitively and the tree will still inspirit the piece that has been taken. If a piece of fallen wood is found, that too may still have the tree spirit's energy within it, or the spirit can be invited to share in the new use of this part of its creativity. Offerings of thanks are always left for the tree in return.

Some say that using metal to cut wood (or indeed any plant) insults the spirits. This idea, I believe, comes from an understanding that the faerie lived in these islands before people brought metalworking and they deeply object to the use of any metal, so wands should be cut with flint knives. Talking clearly and respectfully to the spirit is a sound way to address this problem, however, as cutting wood with stone usually creates more of a mess than most trees will put up with. Cutting a wand in a way that dishonours the tree can result in a piece of wood which is dead, devoid of vitality and the wisdom of its source, or can create a wand that is feisty and resentful, more likely to spread antagonism than clarity and harmony.

A wand, then, is not simply a pointing device, but a means of continuing and deepening the relationship between a Druid and the spirit of a tree.

Some wands are carved, the best of these being an exploration of *awen* shared between the tree and the Druid, and invoking perhaps other spirits, ancestral teachers or animals.

Traditionally, a wand is the length between the bent elbow and the bent wrist or the tip of the middle finger.

A wooden staff works in much the same way as a wand. Though not used so much for directing energy, staffs also show relationships between trees and Druids. The Druid carries her staff as a symbol of her connection to that tree, or that species of trees, and a reminder of the wisdom of all trees. The wood is chosen for its unique wisdom and natural lore; the weight and length (traditionally shoulder height) are carefully determined. A staff amplifies our rootedness deep in the earth, our arms open wide to the beauty of the skies as the branches of a tree, the stability of the trunk reflecting the core of our physical being.

Why is any tool needed to direct energy and intention?

It isn't. An outstretched finger or the gesture of an open hand are equally potent. The dagger or wand, and at times the staff, are simply different ways, offering a different flow, the added influence of other spirits, increasing the potential of our ritual dance and creative expression.

OFFERINGS

An essential aspect of the Druid tradition is understanding the art of offerings. While tools are all optional extras, there is always a need to make appropriate offerings to the spirits of those around us. Nobody, whether a tree, a dog, your mother or the blackbird which sings at dusk perched on your garden wall, enjoys a relationship that does not include a mutual and appropriate exchange of energy.

So, when we are inspired, it is necessary to offer our thanks in return. While simple awe and appreciation go a tremendously long way, it is always sound to know of ways of expression in more concrete forms. Naturally, this is about the creative result of the inspiration we've been given. A spirit inspires us and in return we offer with thanks the poem, the song, the painting, the dance, whatever we have created with that inspiration. That same poem may then be read to a gathering, be published or offered to someone else as a gift of love or teaching, but most importantly we have also given it as an offering to the source that inspired us.

It may be, of course, that it is utterly inappropriate to offer the expression of the creativity back to the spirit. It may be awkward to stand on the cliff in the evening breeze and make our presentation on corporate ethics with overhead projector to the sun as it sets golden over an indigo sea's horizon; instead, we bring back to the cliff our gratitude and we take to work the beauty of the sunset. Our inspiration can be turned into creativity poured into a relationship elsewhere, into success, clarity or any other breakthrough that is not directly related to the inspiring source. Yet it is spirit that inspires, so it is the 'spirit' of our offering that really matters. Being open to see, to hear, to understand, we gather clues as to what form our offerings of thanksgiving might take and we channel our inspiration to create such gifts.

Many Druids will carry with them at all times an offering pouch. In this will be a blend of herbs, seeds, nuts, dried petals or berries, little stones or shells; the mixture is unique to the individual, to the place where he lives, to the season of the year. In autumn a pouch will likely carry grains of the harvest, while through the winter there will be nuts and dried beans, in springtime seeds, and in summer flower petals. Herbs are used a great deal – those that are important to the person, that she uses in her daily or spiritual life, that she has grown herself or gathered from the wild. Such a pouch is a supply of offerings that are a symbolic gift, a way of expressing thanks, honour and respect whenever necessary.

In impromptu rituals, a handful of the pouch mix can be scattered to the wind, left beneath a tree, placed on an altar or thrown into the river. It is important that nothing in the mixture will be poisonous to local wildlife, that no seeds will germinate but those that are native to the local environment and that if outside, no trace of the offering will be left after as little time as a day or so.

My favourite pouch mixture is hazelnuts, sunflower seeds, dried rose petals, catmint and motherwort. This offers the little creatures something to nibble on, together with an offering of the love, tranquillity, healing, creativity and laughter which is my own relationship with the plants and herbs I've included.

In a more formal or planned ritual, it is possible to plan carefully what kind of offerings to bring. The importance of leaving no trace, most especially nothing non-biodegradable, behind at any sacred place, is paramount. Flowers are perfect offerings, but not if they've been taken from the local environment where perhaps it is more fitting that their beauty remains uncut. Bread, fruit and nuts are offerings that the spirits of place will appreciate.

Offerings that are given into the fire, to be transformed into essence as gifts to the ancestral spirits and spirits of place and to the gods, need simply to be burnable. Some offerings are complex creations, scented with oils, with an intention crafted, carved and sown into them or written or painted onto them. Others are simple handfuls of herbs. The nature of an offering is entirely dependent on the nature of the ritual and the individual's journey.

Making offerings on a daily basis to an altar we care for in a regular ritual of thanksgiving is a wonderful way of establishing and deepening a relationship with spirit. Such offerings are the same as any offerings in that it is the gift of spirit to spirit that is the key. Keeping a vase of fresh flowers on the altar is one way of doing it. Having an offering bowl for bread or a little of a main meal that can then be left for the local wildlife or the compost heap is another well-used idea.

So, *nothing is necessary* for ritual but the flow of *awen*. We open ourselves to our spirit core, reaching to perceive and touch the sacred around us, and inspired by the power and beauty of spirit, we offer our thanks in exchange, according to natural law, the expression of our creativity, the continuing flow.

the guiding
FORM

THE beauty of Druidry is in the fluidity of its expression. As a spiritual philosophy and an oral tradition based on the art of relationship, oak tree to tomcat to pebble to human, spirit to spirit, honouring the ever-changing tides and cycles of life, to have a set liturgy of rituals would be anathema. Freedom of spiritual expression is paramount, for without it the tradition would stagnate in just the same way that other spiritualities have, losing its vitality with its flexibility, losing its relevance with its connection and presence, letting go into the constraints of an accepted and established design.

Freedom is easier to grasp, however, if we are aware of the boundaries. A child is able to learn uninhibitedly if it knows the edges of its safe territory. So it is that, over different periods of time, ritual forms have developed in the Druid tradition. Because of the diversity of modern practice, however, these rites cover quite a spectrum.

The Orders and individuals who find inspiration within the Druidry of the eighteenth-century revival, some of whom have a clear history back to that period and links (if less distinct) that head yet further into the past, are often working with rituals that reflect this influence. During the last century especially, the Mystery schools of ancient Greece and Rome, of Egypt and India, added their colour to the tradition, with the philosophies of Qabbala, Theosophy and the occult Golden Dawn.

These Orders work in a way which is firmly structured and hierarchical, reflecting what they perceive to be relationships in the natural world. Like most of the wisdom schools, they use an initiatory system, where instruction takes the student through grades of initiation that allow him access to further sources of knowledge, further doorways into the Mysteries. The rituals are scripted and carry a good deal of ancestral energy after many years of use; participants take roles such as Swordbearer, Pendragon and Presider.

The 'Universal Druid Prayer' *(see page 38)* is a clear expression of this thread of modern Druidry. Replacing 'Spirit' with 'God' and 'Creation' with 'goodness' takes the prayer into a form used by many of the older Orders.

In the 1960s Druidry found an expression that carried a good deal of folk influence. The 'hippy' culture of peace and love, free festivals and folk music, the laidback edges of society that questioned materialism, in some ways attuned with the tenets of Druidry very easily, and smaller modern Orders still promote this way of life.

In many ways their ritual form is at the other end of the spectrum from that of eighteenth-century Druidry, having very little structure at all. Folklore and folk music imbue these ceremonies with the colours and stories of old rural culture. While there may be a few key figures in the rite, guiding its course from a beginning when enough are gathered to a natural closing point, it is seldom that any part of it is scripted or preplanned.

The vast majority within the Druid tradition, however, practise somewhere in the centre ground between these two extremes. Reaching back through the last 200 years and more, exploring the medieval literature and diving into the pre-Roman millennia of the British Isles, Druidry is now practised very much as a tradition that honours its own past, starting with the bedrock of spiritual consciousness, our connection with the powers of the natural world, of the land, seas and skies, and our own basic drives of survival, fertility and stability. Finding its inspiration deep in its ancient roots, it draws that current of energy through its own evolution and growth into a clearly modern spirituality, bringing with it along the way the sticky sparkles of light that have been others' inspiration and creativity through the ages.

Druid ritual is, then, in the main stream of the tradition, a blend of forms, of silence and prayers, fluidity and structure which leaves the individual free to explore his own relationship with both the outer environment and the inner environment within sacred space. Different groups might pick up on different ideas, yet still the basic form remains the same.

What I have done for this chapter is go through Druid rituals from various branches of the tradition, both those I have studied and those I have attended or read, and I have explored the underlying significance of each step.

The following is a guiding form of ritual practice in modern Druidry that is a weave of all these, together with my own. It is offered not as an inflexible structure, but a possible source of inspiration.

FINDING OUR FEET

The hardest part is what we must do before a ritual begins. Clarifying our intention, our need or desire to perform the ritual, is the guiding force, and the more consciousness we have on this level at the outset, the easier will be the flow of the whole ceremony.

The following questions can guide us. Some responses will be easy, the answer being inherent in the overt intention, while others will seem harder to grasp. The answers don't need to be of equal weight, as the focus will often be more specific, intended to make or acknowledge a profound shift in one area of our life, our society, our world. Being thoroughly down to earth and realistic about the answers is always helpful, while remembering that, through the web of life energy, as spirit we are all connected: every thought, word and action shivers out across the web.

It is important not to be altruistic in a ritual intention as the inspiration and flow must come through us and nourish us if we are to perform the ritual effectively. We begin then with the question about ourselves:

❧ What will this ritual give to me?
❧ What will this ritual do for the person it is held for [if applicable]?

* What will this ritual do for my community?
* What will this ritual do for the local environment?
* What will this ritual do for the planet?

With the intention clear, the location set and any preparation on the ritual form completed, when the time is right we can head out for the venue. Once there, it is important to spend a while doing no more than simply settling, feeling the atmosphere: arriving.

When we feel collected enough to begin, the first step is the centring process *(see page 53)*. This exercise takes our consciousness inwards to feel the centre of our being, to glimpse our spirit strength, and in doing so to understand our own sacred nature. Becoming aware of our own energy, our presence in the here and now, our intimate space, we affirm our personal *nemeton* or sanctuary, that place within which we change and grow, wherein lie our thickest blocks and our most potent relationships.

It is important not simply to centre quickly, sense the *nemeton*, then get on with the ritual, but to spend time in the intimate space. As it becomes more familiar, comfortable and flexible, it is easier to reach the moment of being fully prepared; while we are learning the art of ritual, or when life has shaken our very roots, remaining in the glow of our soul *nemeton*, our sanctuary, is profoundly beneficial and a powerful way of preparing for any rite.

Conscious of our own *nemeton*, centred within it, we draw our awareness to the earth beneath our feet, reaching up for the skies above, feeling the energy flow, the breeze on our skin, the tides of our living.

SPIRITS OF PLACE: THE GUARDIANS

Before any ritual is performed it is essential to call upon the guardian spirits of the place where it is to be held. This is not a formality born of a polite English mentality; if the spirits of place don't wish our rite to take place they will simply disrupt it, either in a way that we are aware of, so that the rite must be called off or relocated, or in some way whereby the effects of the ritual are not what was hoped for. So the first thing we do is to ask the guardians if they will allow us to perform the rite in their environment. Doubts and dilemmas must be addressed, as already discussed.

In asking the guardians' permission, it is entirely unnecessary to stumble over complex poetic invocations and declarations. Simple English is sufficient. Often in the tradition statements are made three times, so something like this might be used:

Hail, Guardian Spirit of this place!
Hail, Guardian Spirit of this sacred place!
Hail, Guardian Spirit of this place!
We come here in peace and with clear intent.
We come here to [intention].
And we ask, in peace and with respect, that you might accept our presence.
Hail, Guardian, accept our presence!
Guardian, we ask you to accept our presence.

Speaking of the ritual intent is important here, but we are not talking to all those gathered for the event, simply the guardian of the place. Of the three levels of communication we use in ritual, then, the first two are important here: speaking spirit to spirit, where words are not so necessary because energy is the main medium of communication, and speaking to our own subconscious. Spirit will respond through the vibration of energy, the atmosphere of the place, though those who are able may see or hear an answer more clearly. The response from our own subconscious tells us how we are feeling deep down about performing the ritual, and this emotional feedback needs to be acknowledged. A negative tremor within may not mean that we must call off the ritual (a stronger reaction will indicate clearly if that is the case), but may offer us a distinct impression of the internal fears that are being addressed by doing it.

Inviting a guardian spirit to *participate* in a ritual may not be a clever idea. The guardians are protective entities with a potent ability to hold and direct energy. While they may be excellent bouncers, they can be wholly disruptive party guests.

 Ritual

THE CALL FOR PEACE

Calling for peace in a Druid ritual is a tradition with a long history. Affirming that there is peace on many levels, internally and externally, the Call works through the psyche, the community and the world beyond. It is a way of assuring that the rite is celebrated without disruption.

We can imagine that in the days of our ancestors, when ritual was performed to make a legal contract, to join families in marriage or settle land disputes, perhaps to bring together fighting tribes or clans, perhaps during times of crisis when levels of stress were acute, the need to declare peace was important. The role of the Druid was and still is to find these places of sanctuary within which changes can be made.

In some circumstances the Druid's words will establish peace. Where this is not possible, such as where the politics are fraught and protestations determined, the rite must be reformulated or taken elsewhere.

While any words can be used, the traditional ones are along the following lines.

Walking from her place in the circle to face the four directions in turn and ending by facing (as if calling to) the centre, the Druid calls:

May there be peace in the North!
May there be peace in the South!
May there be peace in the West!
May there be peace in the East!
May there be peace throughout all the worlds!

Sometimes the peace is called by walking around the circle, beginning in the north or the east and moving on clockwise from there. The order given here allows the Druid to draw into the air or the earth, seen or unseen, the lines of a cross, north–south, then west–east. This focuses the power of the prayer, rooting it in the centre of the circle from where it shines out, creating the encircled equal-armed cross of the pre-Christian culture which symbolizes the wholeness of creation.

DEFINING THE TEMPLE

With no traditional building that serves as a shrine, a temple or church in Druidry, the sanctuary is created by the intention. Celebrating the powers of creation, whatever the weather, more often than not the floor of the temple is the grass, the leafmould, the sand or rock of Mother Earth, while the ceiling is the sky above, its colours, clouds, the stars and moon.

Some rituals require the walls of the temple to be high, impenetrable, inflexible, the sanctuary to be absolute. In these rituals, the Druid might call the spirits around and ask that they encircle the place:

Sacred Ones, spirits of the trees that stand around us here, dryads and devas, all you who have heard our intention, I ask with respect, encircle us now, branch reaching branch, leaf touching leaf, roots beneath our feet entangling, that our Grove may be strong, a nemeton of inspiration, reverence and learning. In the name of the Gods whose power we both breathe, I ask that this be so.

In a stone circle, the spirits of the stones might be called upon. Heather or other plants, local waterways or the wind spirits may be asked for their co-operation. Where the spirits of place are very strong, it is possible that no temple will remain intact *unless* the dryad or stone is a principal architect in its making.

Sometimes the circle created by the trees, stones or other spirits resident and holding the energy within the chosen place may be sufficiently strong. Usually, though, a circle is then cast by the Druid in person. This shows a clear intention to detach the temple space from the surrounding world, creating a 'bubble' within which there is absolute safety. The ritual is not affected by the happenings beyond its bounds and the world around is not affected by the upheavals taking place within the ritual space.

A circle may be cast using a sacred knife, a wand or an outstretched finger. Here the Druid is literally cutting the threads that connect the circle with the web of spirit. For a circle which does not need to be so drastically removed, the Druid's intention might be simply to block the flow that travels along the threads, often using a barrier of brilliant energy, light or dark.

The Druid will call upon her source of inspiration for this task. A winter deity might cut the threads with some sharp knife of frost; a goddess of the dark womb of creation might offer her gift of black universal void that nulls the connectedness; a deity of sun or dancing flame may offer his power as a barrier of golden light; a sea spirit might draw a circle of indigo or the undine of a stream a silver blue line through which nothing can pass. The Druid may say:

Hail, Spirit of the Sacred Stream, you who sparkles with beauty through my body, you whose laughter is music to all beings, bringer of life! Lend me your power, walk with me as I cast this Circle. Let nothing cross this line of shimmering blue potency, let nothing cross this line of shimmering blue, in the name of the ancient water Gods of our Ancestors, let nothing cross this line of shimmering blue. So may it be.

If anyone in the circle wishes to leave it during the ritual, the person who cast the circle must be asked to create a doorway through which the other can pass. This is done by requesting that the spirits who created the circle make a temporary doorway, which is closed again securely once the person has left. If not, the circle's integrity will be stretched or broken and the spirits dishonoured. Performing a powerful ritual in a cracked circle or one where the spirits are unhappy can leave those within the ceremony confused, unsettled, shattered for many weeks or more.

When a circle is to be closed but not completely set apart, it might be noted that there are certain creatures which can move through the boundaries without apparently affecting the circle's integrity. Cats and owls can move through powerful circles and other meat-eating birds, scavengers and hunters can make their way into less detached temples. Foxes may be curious; dogs often bark furiously. A child young enough to be still bonded fully to a parent (usually less than two years old, but up to four or five with sensitive children) who is within the ritual space can sometimes move through an energy barrier without badly altering it, as if its connection to the parent within the circle is too strong to block.

Some temples, however, do not need to be so removed. Rites of celebration, thanksgiving and community do not require the same level of uncompromising sanctuary as those of healing or transformation. For these rites, the temple may well be in the same place but it is created as a haven of reverence and festivity.

Here the Druid's request for the dryads, devas or stone people, the spirits of place, to create the circle of the *nemeton* temple may be sufficient. Usually the Druid will weave the circle more fully together, however. This might be done simply by all those gathered holding hands in the circle, thereby affirming their presence together. The Druid might walk in and out of them, weaving like a branch of clematis. She might sprinkle flower petals, seeds or grains, herbs or nuts on the earth around the edges of the circle, depending upon the time of year. She might weave the circle with sound, singing the focus into attunement, so that everyone is drawn into one presence. She might use a wand, her staff or an out-stretched finger, declaring the intention of the circle as it is created:

Let all here draw their minds into the presence of their bodies, that thoughts may be melded with flesh, bones and blood, that the spirits of those gathered may be blended in one purpose, one voice and one sacred space. Soul to soul, we weave our Circle, spirit to spirit to spirit, that none may enter this sacred space but those who come in tune with our intention and in peace. Soul to soul, spirit to spirit to spirit. So may it be.

CONSECRATION

In more formal rites or rites held in places which have not been used for sacred work before, the temple circle is consecrated. Where some crisis has disturbed the energy of a place, consecration is also a useful tool for cleansing and calming.

In Druidry we consecrate using the four elements of creation: earth, air, fire and water. The first three are found in the form of incense, where plant matter is burned to give off a pungent smoke. Both incense and water alter the vibration of energy in a sacred space, clearing, cleansing, lifting, settling, quickening or invoking. They can be healing and exorcising, affirming and dissolving. Incense can clarify the mind and can draw us into dream states. Water from different sources has different effects, the saltwater of the sea having more of a cleansing effect than the life-giving energy of fresh water. It should be borne in mind that salt or saline should never be used where it will kill plants or grass.

Incense comes in two forms in the tradition as it is now practised. More commonly it is a blend of dried herbs, resin, bark, berries and oils, an aromatic mixture that is burned on a special easy lighting charcoal disk. While many Druids buy their blends, some create their own, working with the spirits of the plants to ensure the incense is filled with their energy and particular wisdom.

Here are a few recipes (with ingredients in order of quantity, together with a few drops of oil):

For cleansing: Frankincense, rosemary, vervain, petitgrain essential oil
For celebration: Myrrh, benzoin, applewood, yarrow, chamomile, rose petals, honey
For dreaming: Myrrh, sage, sandalwood, lavender, mugwort, jasmine essential oil

Incense is also burned as bundles of dried herbs and leaves tied securely together and lit. Those particularly good for this are sage, pine, bay, rosemary, thyme, lavender and mugwort, but I must emphasize that these herbs have very different effects and a good herbal dictionary and/or magical herbal should be consulted. There should always be a clear understanding of why a certain herb might be used.

When consecrating, the censer is taken to the centre, the altar or the east, and the Druid asks that the incense be blessed. The smoke of the incense is then offered around the circle, first around the edge, then within the circle of those gathered, then around the centre, three circles being walked altogether before the censer is returned to the altar.

The chalice of water is taken to the centre, the altar or the west, where the Druid asks that the water be blessed. When it is charged, humming with the power of spirit, it is taken around the temple in the same way as the incense, the water being sprinkled upon the ground, the altar and all those gathered as the blessings are shared.

A simpler course can be taken if the ritual is less formal or needs to be shorter. Each person creates the dance of his own rite.

THE DIRECTIONS

The next part of the ritual is the honouring of the spirits that inhabit our world. In some traditions the spirits or guardians are invoked or called into the rite, yet the Druidic perception understands that these spirits are already and always with us. Instead of asking for their presence, we offer them our respect, focusing our mind to understand their power, their wisdom and the relationship we have with them. In other words, we reach for the spirit, the sacred, in the four corners of our world, so that we might find inspiration in every part of creation.

The circle is usually divided into the four directions of east, south, west and north. These simple words hold myriad associations for us and these are developed in more and more intricate patterns, enabling us to divide creation into four landscapes, four views of reality. The shared associations of the directions are rooted in the climate and global position of the area where the rite is being performed; practitioners of Druidry world-wide see very different vistas of creation. Because of this, it is understood that there are no official associations; each person honours the spirits that are a part of his own view of the ever-changing world.

The words used might focus on any of the associations we hold; they might be complex or simple. Here are a few examples to play with:

Spirits of the East, powers of waking and of freedom, blackbird song and eagle's flight, sylphs of the wind, breath of life in the rose light of dawn, I ask that you honour this our Circle as we honour you. Witness and inspire this rite. Hail and Welcome!

Spirits of the South, powers of vitality and of beauty, pride of stag and fire of fox, sprites of the sacred flame untamed, courage and heat, I ask that you honour this our Circle as we honour you. Witness and inspire this rite. Hail and Welcome!

Spirits of the West, powers of fluidity and of direction, wisdom of salmon and otter's play, undines of chuckling brook and raging sea, devas that dance with our love and emotion, I ask that you honour this our Circle as we honour you. Witness and inspire this rite. Hail and Welcome!

 Ritual

Spirits of the North, powers of stability and of potential, guardians of earth and ancient stone, creatures of night and fertile soil, badger and mole, silent owl, I ask that you honour this our Circle as we honour you. Witness and inspire this rite. Hail and Welcome!

In some Druid ritual three more directions are added to the four: the skies above, the earth below and the stillness of the centre. In the main, however, these are honoured not as 'directions' but as 'the three worlds'.

SPIRITS OF PLACE: THE THREE WORLDS

Once we have established our perception as one which sees the world as sacred, we honour the spirits of place once again, those spirits that are both holding and fuelling the energy of our temple and of all creation. This time, instead of simply asking the guardian spirit to accept our presence, we offer our respect and reverence. Our *nemeton* is strong; we are searching for inspiration.

Playing on our ancestors' love of threes once more, the three worlds are those of the land, sea and sky. Who the spirits are, swirling, diving, digging, crawling, prowling through the undergrowth and swaying in the wind, will depend of course on where the ritual is taking place. The land may be crabs and tiny sand-flies, the skies filled with the exuberant bickering of gulls, the seas right beside us, washing cool water over the delineation of the circle. In an entirely different location we may look to the purple heather and squat hawthorn, the fox and shy adder, the buzzards and bees, the call of the grouse, the power of the seas lingering as a mist over the hills. Or something like this may be said:

You of this Place, spirits of oak and ash who encircle us here, holly and bramble, nettles and fern, scampering folk of the undergrowth, weasel and mouse, gathering squirrel, all you who are nourished within this place; spirits of the high blue, jay and chaffinch, kestrel and tawny owl, cloud-kin, star folk, all you who look upon us from your place free-moving in the skies; and you of the silver brook that laughs its journey through this forest, swimming people, frog and minnow in the rushes and water weeds, all who drink of the power of your flow;

know that we come in peace, honouring the beauty of your creativity. Share with us the power of divine *awen*. Blessed be as blessed is. May we know it is so.

Or more simply:

You of our Sacred Lands, of the skies that hold us and of the seas that surround us, tooth and claw, feather and fur, root and branch, flipper and fin, earth and sea and sky, may your journey be blessed by the Gods whom we both revere.

Where we have personal relationships with spirits of place, the hedgehog that always comes snuffling through the rite, the owl that roosts in one of the trees, the cats that watch us, the fox or badger, the trees themselves, these folk may be called specifically to share the journey with us.

In some Druid rites, the words of reverence to the three worlds are expressed in the honouring of the directions. Other rituals in the tradition spend less time on the directions, pouring focus into the three worlds. Some parts of the tradition associate only the land with nature spirits, the seas being the world of ancestral spirits and the skies that of the gods. In practice this is understood to be merely a metaphorical model, and most do acknowledge that there is spirit, ancestral energy and deity in all three worlds.

SPIRITS OF PLACE: THE ANCESTORS

Once we have honoured the spirits of place, stretching to understand their essence and power, searching for *awen*, we look to the ancestral spirits of place. These are the spirits of the land beneath our feet.

When we are speaking of the spirit of the trees or animals, we can understand that the 'spirit' might be understood purely as the life essence within, the guiding flow of vitality. When we turn to the ancestors, just whom are we calling to? There are Druids who do see the souls of those who have passed away in the same way as a medium, spiritualist or shaman. Many don't and don't strive to; it isn't a prerequisite of Druid perception. What Druids do hope to achieve is to sense the presence of the ancestors and to learn from that presence.

When we are talking of those ancestors whose feet walked the earth beneath our feet, whose hands, sweat and blood shaped the landscape, we are looking for their wisdom, the stories of their lives that will guide our own. We don't need to hear the voice through the veils; the teaching is in the hedgerow, the quality of the mud, the life of the stream.

The nature of our call may vary, depending on the purpose of the ritual. It may be a thanksgiving, with offerings, or we may be invoking the ancestors, asking for their presence so that their wisdom might inspire us:

Hail, Ancestors, you of this sacred land, you whose breath we now breathe, whose tears have fallen upon this meadow, whose laughter is music lingering in the trees, whose blood has mixed with this blessed soil, honour our rite as we honour you. If you would come in peace and share our intention, join us here that we may learn. Hail and Welcome!

Druidry is a very locally focused tradition, as is every spirituality rooted in a pagan philosophy. It is the spirits of the environment directly around us that we first turn to and honour, for these are the most important relationships. Yet we never lose sight of the global picture and often a call to the ancestors of the land will be to those of our islands as a whole. If we use more abstract words, such as 'ancestors of the land which feeds us', we can extend the prayer, thanksgiving or invocation through the world as a whole.

THE ANCESTORS: BLOOD AND HERITAGE

Our blood ancestors are also honoured within the tradition of Druid ritual. Again, it isn't necessary to invoke these as souls who drift through the veils, whose voices we might hear: our blood ancestors are within our blood. Their stories, their failures and their mistakes, their victories and affirmations, their life experiences all hum in our bones, flowing through the wires of our nervous system, shimmering in the hologramatic core of every cell. This is our DNA. This is evolution. This is the most powerful source of wisdom, if we would listen to it.

The Guiding Form

So, according to the nature of the ritual, we call to our ancestors of blood, drawing our minds in to focus. It must be remembered, too, that blood ancestry is not only those misty folk puttering through romantic days of myth-hued history – ancestors begin with the sharp faces of our parents.

It might be remembered, too, as we creep into the dawning light of a new millennium, that in just 1,000 years we each have somewhere close to 8,600,000,000 *direct* grandparents or forebears. We are all related. So we might say:

Ancestors, you who gave us life, womb to womb, hand to hand, breath to sacred breath in the twine of souls through millennia upon this Earth, accept our thanks for your innumerable gifts. Those you would join us in peace, be welcome here. Share with us in the beauty of our celebration.

Ancestors also come in threes in the tradition: those of the land, those of blood and those of our spiritual heritage. This last group are those who have shared the spiritual and religious beliefs and perspectives that we too hold. They are the Druids of old, the priests of the land back through time, those who have revered the gods we revere. While our blood relatives gave us the gifts of life, our spiritual forebears showed us the beauty of living:

Hail to you, sacred Ancestors, teachers of old, you whose wisdom has passed through the ages, now to touch us with softness of owl's feathers, with clarity of mountain water, with strength of undoubted love. Enter our Circle, come in peace, that we may know the power of your *awen*. So may it be.

There is an exquisite intensity and calm, a certainty of belonging, of soul rootedness and the inherent pride which that engenders, when the spirits of place are also our blood ancestors and also those that have taught us the beauty of living in a sacred manner.

So the sacred *nemeton* is created and ready for the main part of the ritual.

To carry out every part of the ritual form I've given so far could take half an hour. Obviously, where there is not the time, a shortened version can easily be put together by blending elements and invocations, prioritizing what is important and what is appropriate. However we condense or extend the opening of a ritual, though, it must be kept in mind that the creating of sacred space is profoundly important in any rite. Simply making the temple is the heart of spiritual and ritual practice. Our intention, on some level, is always to acknowledge the world as sacred, and it is the creating of a sacred sanctuary which affirms that perfectly.

THE DECLARATION

Once the *nemeton* has been created, the intention of the ritual is again clarified and shared. This is the 'declaration' of a rite, when the Druid announces why it is that everyone has been brought together. Of course, usually everybody knows (though it can be a surprise!), but the declaration turns our attention to the specifics.

Sometimes the Druid will draw the focus even more clearly by saying something such as this, an example taken from a marriage ceremony:

We gather together on this the 29th day of the month of July, the 17th night of Claim Song Moon, in the year of 1999, in the eye of the Sun and upon this hallowed Earth, upon the Isles of Britain, to witness the sacred Rite of Marriage between Helen and Nick. May all who have come know what is done.

The intention was previously stated for the spirit guardian of the locality, so that they would accept and bless the rite; now it is spoken to all who have gathered, in body and in spirit. It is a prayer for guidance, an affirmation of resolve, a confirmation of the goal shared, once again bringing the focus of all those present into the here and now, into 'one purpose, one voice and one sacred space'.

THE GODS

It isn't necessary to work with gods in Druid ritual. As a spiritual philosophy that holds within it so many different religious paths, from the Classical to the

Christian, Nordic to Celtic, the tradition is not primarily about deity, but about our relationship with the spirits of place and the ancestors.

Having said that, the gods are understood to be powers of nature and as such are spirits holding incredible forces, those of thunder, anger, tidal flows, ore, communication, love, fire, death and so on. As sources of inspiration they have a wealth of resources and it is for this reason that they are often invited or entreated to join a ritual. They bring with them *awen*.

The invocation is done in two ways: directly and indirectly. Through the telling of a myth, the gods, legendary heroes and luminaries of our heritage can be painted upon the minds of those listening within a rite. Where there is only the belief that the character is an abstract or construct, the imagination will do its work, allowing the lessons of the tale to seep through the soul and the subconscious, offering its cup of inspiration where it can. Where the gods and heroes are understood to be entities separate from the psyche, powers in their own right, these figures can be invoked directly. When this is done by a Druid it is because he has an effective grasp of the nature of that god. He is building a relationship and knows what it takes to access the god's curiosity, attention, power and co-operation. If he doesn't, either the deity will pay no heed to his invocation or the Druid will find a litany of uncomfortable (and often dangerous) surprises in store for him.

Interacting with the gods is a part of an individual's adventure, if and when he chooses to take it. It is something which is best done alone, or with good guidance. Using myth and story for invocation allows the interaction to be held within the safety of the tale.

The search for inspiration, then, entices us to work with powerful spirits, elementals and deities. Sometimes the purpose of a ritual is about forging such a relationship. Where it is not, the sources of *awen*, the spirits that inspire us, are called at this point to attend and infuse our ritual with their exquisite powers.

As in every part of the ritual, it is better to use down-to-earth language than attempt poetry and lose the impact by stumbling. The poetic colours of an invocation, however, are simply a way of clearly explaining what we see.

Invocations might be something like the following:

To the goddess Bride or Bridget:

Lady of the Eternal Flame, thy priestess calls to thee.
As the flame everlasting burns for thee.
So may your inspiration burn within me,
Through time, sweet Bride, through time.

(KW)

To Woden, the Saxon god:

Hail to Woden, wisest of wights,
Howls of wolves and ravens' cries,
Be sig-runes writ on this bright day!

(AS)

To Cerridwen, the Welsh goddess:

Hail, Dark Power of the Ancient Cauldron,
Stirring the wisdom of soul's unknowing,
Deep within the wilderness of all creation,
May drops of your *awen* brew fall now upon me!

To Llew Llau Gyffes, the Welsh god:

Bright One of the Skilful Hand,
Rising Sun at break of day
Spear of fire, Sun's first ray
Illuminate both mind and land!

(PS)

To the Christian god:

One God of all the Earth,
One God who created us,
One God who redeems us,
One God, come to us and be with us,
Fill us and empower us!

(LD)

THE ACTION

With the sanctuary created, the spirits of creation honoured, our gods and sources of inspiration invoked, what needs to be done in a ritual can be done, whether it is a ritual for change, a rite of passage or a festival celebration. The next section of this book will deal with this central part of the ritual.

THE GROUNDING

At the end of a ritual the winding down process is as important as creating the temple in the beginning. Any benefit gained can be shattered if the closing is done ineffectively or disrespectfully.

The first step of the closing is to ensure that the energy flowing within the circle is indeed still flowing and hasn't got stuck in some crevice of self-negation or distraction. *Awen* must keep moving. If it is, then we will feel revitalized, clear and inspired, perhaps thoughtful, a little tired from the rite, but wholly creative. If it isn't, we might feel 'spaced out', somehow unreal.

When the ritual has been powerful, the need to ground is even more crucial. Simply checking the flow and how we feel may be enough to restore the balance once again. If not, we can return to the consciousness we had before the ritual began. Aware of our own sacred circle of intimate space within the wider circle or filling the circle (if that is appropriate), we can again follow the energy of the earth as it seeps into our body, rising through us like summer sap to spread through our branches, reaching up into the skies, as the energy of the sun is gently absorbed by our skin, tingling, slipping down through our bones and into the earth.

Balanced, centred between earth and sky, we review the ritual, our purpose, the energy we have invoked and the inspiration gained, and we spend the time we need simply letting that current move on into our creative response. Sometimes it is possible and appropriate to pour our inspiration into creativity while still within the ritual space, to dance, sing, write or sculpt, to generate a needed breakthrough, to find a new idea, a new level of healing, whatever it may be. If we must wait, our awareness of the flow will hold and guide our focus until the rite is done, when the energy will pour into the world beyond according to our new *creative* intention.

THE *EISTEDDFOD*

The *eisteddfod* in Druid ritual is the 'official' place for our creativity to be expressed, though the weather, the nature of the rite and every other influence and intention will decide whether and when this is the case.

THE FEAST

The celebratory sharing of the feast affirms that we are in touch with our physical selves and grounds the rite more deeply.

In many Druid rites this feast is of bread and mead. The bread is first blessed with the Druid touching it to the ground and calling to the powers of earth, to those of the dark soil that feeds us, to the goddess of the land who nourishes our crops. Rich words of thanksgiving are often used, those that weave with the course and purpose of the ritual, words that are appropriate too for the time of year. The Druid might speak of the magical alchemy that takes the green wheat through its golden drying and dying process to emerge from the fires as the sacred loaf, the staple food of our culture.

A simple blessing might be something like this:

Mother Earth, in the name of our Gods and the Gods of our Ancestors, we give you thanks. You nourish us body and soul with your gifts of beauty and of abundance. As you honour us with such precious life, so may we honour you. May this bread be blessed.

The mead, often in a traditional mead horn, but otherwise in a drinking bowl or chalice, is then raised to the skies and the powers of nature are called upon as the Druid makes his blessing. Often he will speak of the wild dance of the bees, the nectar of summer's bright and colourful flowers, the sun's fire drawn down through sweetest beauty to inflame the sacred drink of our ancestors.

A simpler blessing would be something like:

Father Sky, in the name of our Gods and the Gods of our Ancestors, we give you thanks. Light of the Sun and blessings of rain fall upon the body of our Mother, bringing forth her gifts. As you honour us with your blessings, so may we honour you. May this mead be blessed.

The bread is then broken and the first part is given back to the earth. Likewise the first sip of mead is poured upon the ground. If there is a fire or ancestral altar, the next part and sip are offered to the ancestors with the invitation:

Feast with us, spirit to spirit!

The key individuals in the rite are then offered a mouthful of bread and a sip of mead with a blessing that is apposite to the ritual. Here are a few ideas:

Eat, that no one may hunger. Drink, that no one may thirst.
May this bread be the first taste of an abundant harvest.
May this mead be fire to warm your heart through the winter.

The feast is then taken around the circle and offered to everyone who has gathered. In this way the blessings of the land and of the ritual are shared.

Though bread and mead are traditional, they can easily be replaced. A non-alcoholic juice may be more suitable at some rituals and one made of local fruit is especially apt. Ale or cider are also used, ideally locally brewed and as strong,

light or dark as the season would find appropriate. Occasionally, where fitting and acceptable, mead is replaced with wine, port or whisky, again preferably locally crafted.

In summertime, when the rituals are blessed with warm sunshine and can drift on for hours, very often after the ritual sharing of bread and mead, the feast is opened out to become a glorious picnic, the *eisteddfod* continuing amidst the food and drink.

THE CLOSING

After the sharing of the feast and the *eisteddfod*'s creativity, the last prayers are said within the circle, with thanks being given to all those whose spirits have inspired the course of the ritual's flow and blessings offered out to the worlds beyond.

The closing of the ritual is in many ways a simple reversal of the process that created it. Each spirit who has been honoured and invited to witness, inspire, bless and protect the rite is once more honoured, this time with thanks. While most of the spirits of place and the powers of nature who have infused the temple with their energy will remain present anyway, as we come to close the ceremony we say our goodbye:

Return to your realms in peace, as in peace you came to honour this our rite. With thanks, in the name of the Gods of our people, and all that we have been, all we are, all we can become, we bid you from this sacred rite, hail and farewell!

Beginning with the gods, then the ancestors of blood and heritage, the ancestral spirits of the land, the spirits of place, the three worlds and the four directions, dryad, devas, the faerie and elementals, all are honoured and given thanks. Nobody can be missed out, for if they are, the energy of that relationship will hold a part of us in that otherworldly place of the ritual, keeping us unsettled and ungrounded.

Spirits of the North, great bear, mighty badger, spirits of earth, we give you thanks for the gifts of strength and endurance that you have brought to our

The Guiding Form

Circle. My Lady of the Womb, may your gifts remain with all who have gathered here this day. We bid you hail and farewell!

Spirits of the West, wise salmon, laughing otter, spirits of water, we give you thanks for the gifts of deep wisdom and fluidity that you have brought to our Circle. My Lady of the Seas, may your gifts remain with all who have gathered here this day. We bid you hail and farewell!

Spirits of the South, proud stag, running fox, spirits of fire, we give you thanks for the gifts of passion and energy that you have brought to our Circle. My Lord of the Wildwood, may your gifts remain with all who have gathered here this day. We bid you hail and farewell!

Spirits of the East, singing blackbird, eagle flying, spirits of air, we give you thanks for the gifts of clarity and far sight that you have brought to our Circle. My Lord of the Rising Sun, may your gifts remain with all who have gathered here this day. We bid you hail and farewell!

The thanksgivings done, the last prayers made, the circle is now ready to be opened, marking the end of the ritual. If the temple was detached by cutting the threads that connect us to all life through the web of spirit, to open the circle the Druid weaves those threads again, walking counter-clockwise around the circle, using the power of her intention. If a barrier of brilliant energy was scribed, the Druid withdraws it as she walks the circle. If the circle was simply woven together, spirit to spirit, in one intention, the counter-clockwise walk can be enough to open it. Hands held in a circle are consciously unclasped. The outside world trickles in.

If other circles were invoked, those made by the dryads and devas, or the spirits of the stones, these will stay firm and true until the Druid, giving thanks, asks that these spirits release their hold. In this way, the shift from the sacred sanctuary of the consecrated circle back into daily life is made a gentle process, step by step.

When a circle is opened, particularly one which has been tightly cast, the shift in energy in extraordinary. Often the temperature drops suddenly, a wash of vulnerability sliding in as we are once more exposed to the energies of a changing

world. At the same time, there's the excitement of being able to take what was done in the ritual and integrate it into our ordinary lives. The inspiration gained starts itching to be used.

The Druid then offers thanks to the guardian spirit of the place and all those seen and unseen who are still gathered around. The last prayers before the ritual is done might sound something like these:

May the Spirits of this Place have been nourished as much as their presence has nourished us. Guardian Spirit, we give you thanks. May your Gods guide and protect you well, the energy of your worlds flowing freely and inspired. Blessed be as blessed is.

This celebration ends in peace as in peace it began. May the wealth of this rite and the blessings we have received go with us all as we depart this place, to nourish, strengthen and sustain us until we meet again.

So may it be!

The words and prayers, invocations and blessings in this chapter are given as a guide. I would recommend that readers use their own ...

THE RITUALS

A man can't plough a field
by turning it over in his mind.

Welsh proverb

rituals for everyday
LIVING

MOMENTS

Living in a sacred manner, our perception of the world as inspirited, powerful and free allows us an awareness of our beauty. We draw from the well of inspiration, drinking deeply the cool pure energy that washes humming through our bones, our veins, our fingertips.

Yet performing ritual once in a blue moon, or occasionally at the weekends and only when there is the time to create a *nemeton* that is cast and consecrated does not lead us into a life that is blessed as sacred. It is the ongoing process of living with those ups and downs that demand a response, that demand our attention, that guides us ever deeper into a perception that is sacred. It is the simple acts, the moments of ritual, that give us the stable ground in which to grow.

The spontaneous need to give thanks for the beauty of the clouds that stretch like paint flung wide across the skies, the tender need to acknowledge a moment of achievement within the swirl of only just coping, the very real need to ask for help when mist obscures the path ahead, these are times when ritual in its simplest forms can be used so very poignantly.

Some ritual moments are not so impromptu; planned, they become a part of our usual routine. Affirming our beliefs, asserting our desires, we might light a candle when we rise in the chill of morning, we might offer a clear gift of thanksgiving before we eat, touch the frame of the door as we enter, asking the spirits for acceptance, scatter offerings into the river as we cross over the bridge.

The reason we do this is not to complicate our lives further with things to be done. We are simply honouring the spirits of place, giving thanks and making requests, and in doing so we deepen our connection and our relationship with the environment in which we live. All life is sacred and it is only our limited perception of it as sacred that constrains the beauty of our living, compromising our relationship with the world that supports us. So ritual, as a means of allowing us to see the sacred, is not something to do now and then, but a practice to live with.

Seeing the spirit that is the creative energy of everything around us brings us beauty, intensifying life, adding zest and sparkle, opportunities for learning, for serenity and stability, nourishment and joy; acknowledging the spirit offers us inspiration and love.

INTUITIVE RITUAL

Even where we aren't creating a ritual using the elements described in the previous chapter, the basics are still essential: the respect we offer to the spirits of place and our sources of inspiration. In fact, the essence of any momentary ritual is simply that – we create a sacred moment by stopping the movement of our bodies and minds until we are present, just pausing for a while. Listening, watching, witnessing both the world around us and the world within, scenting what has brought us walking into this moment, without over-analysis ... For a moment we are simply in the 'here and now'.

Sometimes that pause is enough. Overwhelmed and amazed, we can offer our thanks. The words can flow, as we intuitively offer the gratitude and awe of our souls. As ever, it is important to be clear to whom we are speaking. Being aware of where our inspiration is coming from always guides us.

Such a moment's focus can bring us into a stillness, balanced and soul naked. When it doesn't, the exercise of centring within the sanctuary of our intimate space is beautifully useful. The more easily and quickly, the more effectively we can do this, the more valuable we will find the skill. When the world is swirling around us, knowing our boundaries yet not using them so much defensively as with a consciousness of self, we are able to walk with confidence, to stand firm, to dance, however wild the storm might be.

Safe space might be further affirmed for momentary rituals with simple comfort items. A fat cushion, a cup of hot chocolate, and the circle of our own *nemeton* is made even stronger. It is important to remember that making a place sacred does definitively *not* mean detaching it from our own sense of beauty, truth and inner calm. An old teddy bear may be the key ingredient. It is easy to get lost in images of incense and highbrow ritual tools, reaching for validation, and to forget the real point. We make ritual for ourselves, for our own souls and our own happiness, growth and peace, whatever that may take.

So, pausing in the swirl of life, affirming the sanctity of our own body's *nemeton*, we can then move through the three levels of communication that are ritual. With clear intent, we reach out, our own sacred centre opening to the source of our inspiration, spirit to spirit, through that mystical blend of vulnerability and divine power that is our physical mortality and our spirit core. Allowing the energy to flow through us, guiding it with our emotions and/or our bodily movement, we reach within ourselves, touching, shifting or affirming the subconscious perspectives of our own minds. Waking to the environment and the community within which we live, we can direct the flow of our communication outwards, allowing our rite to affect the worlds around us. Our offerings are made and the rite is done.

DAILY MEDITATION

The soles of my boots slip on the wet ground, grating on pebbles, puddles briefly stirred with the paler mud my steps unsettle, and I wonder at how quickly yesterday's ice has melted. The grey light of dawn is chilly in my lungs. I'm glad to reach the top, but then I always am, even in the summer when most days I am here long after the sun has risen, for each day the view across the land fills my soul. Each day I watch the turning of the year, the sheep in the meadows, the fields changing their colours from dark brown mud to luscious green to golden wheat swaying in the breeze.

As I sit, snug in the oak roots that serve as my chair, I watch the rooks in the high branches of a distant patch of grey woodland, leafless and still, and I listen to the subtlety and sharpness that are the voices of early spring, look at the soft mauves in the land.

Beneath me, beneath the sleepy oak, the earth is humming. I can feel it in my fingertips and it causes a silent smile to move over my lips. Gazing at the horizon, without thoughts, waiting, my eyes rest upon the hawthorn over which the sun rose yesterday.

Waiting, it feels as if everything is waiting. And when the first light breaches the hill, like liquid gold seeping into the far meadow, laughter rises in me as I whisper, 'My Lord, yet closer you rise to the east, yet closer to the equinoctal marks, bringing us summer, hail my Lord, hail my Lord, bringing us to summertime, warming the earth ...'

Creating time in our lives for a daily meditation is beneficial on so many levels. The simple act of dedicating time to our own tranquillity and growth is often a transforming step when more often we are evading ourselves, caring for others (be it our children, our clients, our supervisors...). We might begin with just five minutes, enough to light a candle and make a simple prayer. Twenty minutes is better, allowing us to move through one cycle of attention, and any longer will give us an opportunity for more extended ritual practice. Ideally the time should be put aside on a daily basis, at a regular hour, giving our bodies an opportunity to adjust gently and expect the period of stillness. If we make it at a time when we'll be struggling not to fall asleep, we will lose the opportunity. It is better to put aside a few minutes of our prime time instead.

As in most traditions, meditation in Druidry is the art of finding the calm beyond the chattering of our thinking-talking minds. It is the step beyond focus and clear concentration when we are utterly absorbed, when, released from the usual need to respond, we exist in the gap between the past and the future, in the pure simplicity of presence. In Druid meditation, however, we aren't seeking to transcend our experience or awareness of physicality. Listening, watching, sitting, stepping in bare feet, we are absorbed in the nature of the worlds within which we live, worlds richly coloured by the creativity of spirit. A tree or leaf, a stone or gem, a candle or the setting sun, an altar of any kind that inspires our own souls can act as a focus, an expression of physical creativity that is also a doorway through which we can meander into the essence of its spirit.

This daily meditation is a time for acknowledging where we are, for giving thanks and centring, reinforcing our view of the world as sacred, strengthening the positive and so finding the courage to address the negative. It allows us to process life without analysing. It reminds us that we are free.

THANKSGIVINGS

There's a dampness in the wind that seems to cling to my face almost as if I were walking through a high mountain mist. Yet the air is clear, so fresh it draws my attention down along the wind's flow as if I might catch a glimpse of all it were taking with it. I breathe in and resolve to carry on, climbing carefully over fallen wood, the twigs and branches torn down, the forest floor covered with debris.

My heart is in my mouth. So far I've come across no serious damage, but I've not reached the worst of it and I carry on, half longing for and yet half dreading the intense quiet that will come when this tail end of the storm has passed us by.

I can feel the disruption before I see the old oak, my skin suddenly cold, the hairs on my arms like antennae. My tears are already falling as I step into the devastation, this great giant slain, and I lean over its body, utterly overwhelmed, my tears slipping onto the deep grey ridges of bark.

Enough ... Whose voice it is doesn't really matter. Mine, perhaps, or that of the old dryad, maybe a spirit guide. But I know it is right. My grief is expressed; it's time to move on. And as I open my eyes, I catch a glimpse of a sapling, bathed for a moment in clear golden light, a break in the clouds. I draw my focus into my centre and feel the strength of my spirit, the circle of my *nemeton* warm in the cool wet wind, and as I look again I hear the young tree's spirit, calling through the uncertainty, a sweet clear song of anticipation, of fresh new life. I push the tears from my eyes and walk towards it, stepping over the shattered branches.

Crouching beside it, I leave my offerings, dried herbs and rose petals from my pouch, tears falling still easily from my cheeks to the ground. I touch the tree's soft young leaves and listen to its song.

A good many of our momentary rituals are cries for help, at times when the forces of nature are too turbulent to deal with, and we tumble with the breaking waves, hitting the ground, gasping for breath. Yet it is those same powers around us that offer us the most exquisite highs, the utterly exhilarating journeys, the greatest teaching of the powers of love and death, of the abundant harvest and the winter night's storm. Not all lessons are easy. The greatest are often given with the most destruction.

Giving thanks for all that offers us strength and learning is a key part of ritual practice in the Druid tradition. Honouring the power of nature, even when there is difficulty, the Druid will seek out the creative potential. He doesn't deny the pain, the muck, the horror that does exist, but he acknowledges the life force that is the inspirational charge, allowing the *awen* to flow into his soul, using its pure energy for his own creativity.

As such, Druidry is a powerfully optimistic philosophy, always reaching for the power that is inspiring, acknowledging the spirit essence that is connected to all existence through the web of life energy. As we give thanks for the warmth of the sunshine, the force of the wind, the beauty of the moon, the blind flood of love, the miracle of fertility, we are offering the web our positive energy of gratitude, honour and respect, and so feeding all creation.

All at once I realize I have been fighting in vain. What a waste of energy. Slowly I breathe out the sigh I've been holding on to, relaxing every muscle in my shivering body, releasing the tension that has been wrapping me up so very tightly. I drop my shoulders, lift my face into the rain.

And for a moment, eyes closed, I listen.

Slowly, the clamour of the traffic all about me, the people pushing by me, the car horns and muffled music, my remonstrating mind, seem strangely to come together in some extraordinary symphony. Stretching out my arms I start to laugh, calling inside me to the gods of the skies, the cloud-kin, the dark thunder spirits, every creature around me.

And as the beauty of the moment bubbles up through me, there standing in the rain in Leicester Square, twirling, soaked, letting go into its cleansing city-sticky torrent, I notice I've been joined by two more souls, then three and more, umbrellas abandoned, mouths open in laughter, open to the skies.

Thank you!

  Ritual

Giving thanks for food is a tradition that many of us have been brought up with, regardless of which spirituality was part of our childhood. In Druidry, it is a key part of daily practice, together with honouring the spirits of place who inhabit the buildings and land we call home.

Every meal, from the elaborate ritual feast to a snack *en route*, is prepared with respect, the life force that flows through it being sincerely honoured. For this reason most modern Druids are vegetarians and a good number are vegan, believing it to be unnecessary in our gentle culture to take another's life for our own nourishment and pleasure.

Many Druids, acutely conscious of the environmental impact of consumerism and wishing to care for their own bodies as well as the earth, will eat only food that is healthy and rich in its own spirit potency. Processed food is so far from its original ingredients, so chemically altered, it is hard to connect to the nourishment of its source. If a good part of our diet is fresh raw fruit and vegetables, still vibrant with life and filled with the natural enzymes that are the sparkle of food energy, not only are we still in contact with the creative source but the amount that we need to eat is greatly reduced.

Acknowledging where our food comes from is an important part of giving thanks. Sugar snaps from Ghana, bananas from Guatemala, avocados from Israel are all foods that have been nourished by very different soils, worked by the sweat and prayers of different peoples, blessed by their gods, on land loved and abused. These foods have been grown in the fields of their ancestors and we are touched by these spirits when we eat their crops.

Being conscious of what we are eating allows us to make more informed decisions about what to avoid, such as genetically modified products, artificial additives, unnecessary sugars, sweeteners and salt. In doing this we not only keep ourselves healthier, honouring our own bodies, but we also stop unknowingly supporting environmentally damaging industries. Where food is naturally, organically grown, there has to be a clear relationship between the farmer and the land; it a bond that is co-operative, respectful and not abusive, and that honour is reflected in the food that is produced.

Blessing our food, calling to the powers of the land, we reach to the spirits of all those whose lives and energy have been a part of its growth. We reach to the spirit of the plants (and animals) that we eat, with respect and with profound thanks. In this way, we not only take in the physical value of the food, but also share the strength and beauty of its life force, its creative essence: spirit to spirit, we are nourished.

Mother Goddess, you of the rich and fertile soil
Father of the Skies, divine eye of perfect light
Your dance of power, its brilliance, dark mystery
Is held within this feast, *awen* like mother's milk
May we know what we eat.
May the spirits be honoured!

With survival being one of our main three drives (the others being sexuality and familiarity), food and shelter are vital keys to life. I have spoken of the former, but what of shelter?

While many of us are not unfamiliar with giving thanks for food, honouring the spirits of our home environment is not so usually a part of our conditioning. Many Druids will have an altar or other focus at the doorway to their home which acts as a reminder to honour the spirits. By this I mean all those ancestral and local spirits of place whose energy still hums in the stone and the earth, whose stories still linger in the air that we breathe. It is their energy which gives a home its atmosphere, its comfort or insecurity. It is their energy which makes a home nourishing or detrimental, healing or unstable. A house where there is sickness is often one where the spirits of place have been abused and dishonoured.

Such an altar may be elaborate or simple, a rock for offerings, a cairn of beautiful and special stones, a string of old acorns, an old horseshoe, or any other object which may have infused within it a dozen meanings, bringing the magic of fertility, protection or stability. An altar inside the house might have fresh flowers, memorabilia of the ancestors, photographs, stones, cleansing water. Its key purpose is always to serve as a focus, a reminder to honour the spirits of place.

It isn't always enough just to make offerings. Some house spirits want a place tidy and clean, some hate too much order but dislike the dust even more. Sometimes a change is never accepted and the spirits are unsettled until a tree has been planted to replace one cut down, or a partition removed, an old well reused. Most often, it is the very real actions of daily living that make the difference, not the poetry of our prayers.

Where the spirits are happy, their dance of being will fill a place with inspiration.

ASKING FOR HELP

Many rituals of everyday life are far from planned or routine. As the bubbling currents of reality swirl and flow, eddies catching us unawares, many rituals are pleas for help from the midst of crisis, desperate cries for inspiration from the chaos of tumbling, falling white water. However we believe our lives are patterned, by whatever design of fate or coincidence, when circumstances are oppressive most of us will reach out to those unseen powers who seem to be holding the threads of destiny. The powers of nature, elementals and gods, a sentience of the universe beyond human perception, somebody, surely, must understand what is going on, someone out there must know how to press the STOP button and EJECT... But so often it is as if the gods take not a blind bit of notice. Then any faith we might be clinging to starts to falter as our self-negating beliefs are once again confirmed.

However, strangely, sometimes our prayers do work, the storm subsides, the waters still. Most often we aren't entirely sure what made the difference. Yet by bringing our focus into the sanctuary of our own circle, the centre shining, our spirit in balance, the chaos we perceive does transform into clarity. Calm within our invulnerable core, we send out different messages to the world around us, and the world responds, untroubled and clear.

Reaching out to the powers of nature with our physical body, we hit the physicality of creation. Reaching out with our minds, we face ourselves, the rigid inflexibility and the flimsy plasticity of our own attitudes and assumptions. Hurling our emotions at the world, the energy ricochets, splashing back over us. Yet when we reach out with our spirit, it is spirit we touch, the essence of life.

When we can't find that clarity, our vision too disrupted by the crisis around us to centre ourselves in the circle of our intimate space, it is through our call for inspiration that we are guided. The strength of our intention to see makes the difference. And it is the trees, the breeze, the face of a flower, the touch of affection, the call of an unseen bird, spirits who have no investment in our blinkered lack of self-esteem, in the devastation of the world not viewed as sacred, that lead us to a state of calm. Wherever the *awen* flows, there is a source of inspiration.

The car blew up on the motorway. He turned to me, frowning, and I woke from my snooze to his uncertainty. Smoke was escaping from the sides of the bonnet, losing itself in the wind past our windows. We were two hours from our destination, already late. Pulling up on the verge, smoke billowed from the car, no longer dispersing in the speed of the wind. It smelled as if the whole machine were furiously melting. We looked at each other, wondering whether to get angry, upset. I called to my Lady.

A crow cawed from the woodland across the field. I stretched. We smiled and sat down to wait for the rescuers to arrive.

In the gravel along the verge there were some extraordinary fossils.

We were losing communication. Something I had said had triggered some old pain, and now I was talking to a grey blank screen. He was staring at me as if I were someone he barely recognized, projecting the other woman onto my face – his mother, his ex-girlfriend, all those who had tossed his trust to shatter on the stones. Quite suddenly I knew that we'd reached a dead end.

I turned to the window, seeking guidance, the words of my prayers seeping through my soul, into the sunlight that flickered through the summer branches of the oak, touching the paving of the courtyard outside. Patterns of gold on grey. Its silence reflected the moment around me.

When our eyes met, with all my affection, my pride dismantled, I smiled, allowing that sunlight to flow through my face, flickering through the leaves of my uncertainty.

And he nodded. We laughed at the frailty of our confidence.

 Ritual

The process is the same as in any ritual: we centre in our own space, finding the clarity of our sanctuary, then, watching, listening, stepping carefully forward again, we balance our priorities by understanding what of our conscious and subconscious beliefs the situation is provoking us to express, what is important, what can be changed.

Where the beliefs are easily adjusted, priorities rearranged, the shift can be simple. Where we are dealing with basic paradigms that have chained and weighed us down for what seems like forever, the process needs more energy. The Druid will focus, diving, soaring, reaching with all she is, deep into the powers that are holding the situation or out to her own sources of pure inspiration, asking those spirits to awake to her, enchanting them to understand her perspective, to know what she needs help with. She may believe she knows exactly what must happen, but all her beliefs she lays to one side as she calls for guidance ...

My Lord, you who know the power of these things, you who have guided me as you have guided my ancestors for many thousands of years, watching over every trade and every coin exchanged, be with me here, know my intent, guide me, inspire me to know how to pay this bill!

It is an important point that in Druidry we *do* let go of our expectation, our sense of what we believe will be the best way forward. Druidry is not a tradition which primarily uses 'magick': the craft of consciously creating change by force of will. The changes that occur in Druidic practice are based on inspiration, the problem being offered to the powers of nature, the spirits who hold the energy and patterns of the environment within us and around us (including ourselves, our own sacred spirit). It is through the inspiration we are given that the solution is revealed, together with the energy to make it happen, the current of *awen* flowing into creativity.

Magick carries with it the profound risk that we manifest for ourselves that which we don't really want – though we believed we did. We are able to get the girlfriend, the car, the job, save the child's life, adjust someone's perspective, even when that change is not in tune with the flow of *awen*, but lessons can come brutally when we force a situation that wouldn't naturally have occurred. And magick is not something only done by the well-trained mage; we all create change in our environment by the force of our will, fuelled by the energy of our emotion, our grief and fear, our lust, anger, envy and pain.

By calling for inspiration, however, we are calling to the creative spirit of all those involved, all those who are connected and will be affected by a change in the situation. By calling to the spirit essence we are not working with the threatened and defensive part of our psyche, but with the invulnerable centred core. The inspiration emerges from the place where we are all connected, sharing a sacred purpose.

In a situation that is traumatic, whether because some accident has just occurred, or because prayers are asked for quickly, or because suddenly we can't cope with an ongoing situation illness, the way forward is always to stop, to pause for a moment. Within the intimate space of our own body's *nemeton*, we will find the confidence that alleviates panic and by checking the edges of our intimate space, we can relax into the sanctuary of its circle. Centred in our own spirit, we can then address the flow of negative energy, our own or whatever is spilling into the situation from others. Expressing our own calm reduces the potential damage caused by the energy of panic, rage or fear, within and around us, that confidence inspiring others to mellow too and find their own strength. A relaxed body doesn't need to express the energy of negative emotion: we can't be angry or scared when we are calm.

Although I speak of the spirits as if we can hear their response, word for word, in perfect clarity, the reality is that most of us don't. The common mistake is our believing that this makes a critical difference. It doesn't. On the pavement in the city, the clamour of the rat race all around, when a Druid needing help cries out for inspiration, calling to those spirits who fill his soul with *awen*, he may not hear their voices but he will stop for a moment, and in his listening and watching the worlds around he'll see the wind playing in the leaves of the plane trees, or the shapes of the clouds in the sky above, or the laughter in the eyes of a stranger passing by. And the *awen* flows.

HEALING

Healing in Druidry is about inspiration. Certainly, Druids are less likely to use chemical medications and unnecessary drugs than a person not conscious of the natural flow of life's energy, but the potency of Druid healing does not come from alternative herbal and subtle remedies. The greatest healer is inspiration, to be touching the essence of creative energy and living life to the full and in a sacred manner. So many problems that affect the body and mind are caused by a crisis in our perspective, and the Druid knows that there is no greater motivation to live well than to sip from the cup of *awen*. This is not only relevant in healing ourselves, but offers blessings of change on a social and global level as well.

While we'll look at ways in which we can draw inspiration into situations that need healing through ritual in more depth in Chapter Eleven, there are many more occasions when ritual is required to make a difference in a passing moment of crisis.

When thrown into a need for healing energy, a Druid will often call to her ancestors. So much of that which blocks the flow of healthy life energy are crises that are passed down to us generation after generation. Through our parents' experiences, tears and resignations, their bitterness and fears, they show us the world as they perceive it. Their blindness and weaknesses, passed to them by their parents, are mapped in the genes which they pass on to us. So it is that we repeat the patterns and mistakes of our ancestors until we can consciously see and break the cycle.

Ancestors of the land on which we live also feed us their energies, through the fertility of the soil, their stories held in the stones, in the trees. Their mistakes are crises which we are dealing with now in the same way that generations to come will be coping with the residue and consequences of mistakes we are making now. Calling to our ancestors, those of our bloodline, those of the land and those who hold the teachings and wisdom of our spiritual heritage, we reach for their knowledge and their understanding, for the inspiration that is the flow of energy between us, spirit to spirit. Often, when we are in need of the clarity and confidence that will heal a situation, finding the touch of inspiration from our ancestors is the most poignant course. Offering a prayer of healing to our ancestors, lighting a candle before a photograph, laying a flower by a standing stone or grave, we give positive energy to the whole family line.

As with any spirit, it isn't necessary to hear the voices of those ancestral spirits. Feeling their presence, being aware of their energy, knowing that they are with us, their creativity still expressed in the cut of the land, the stones of the house, a photograph, a painting, the smile that reflects their legacy of genes, is often sufficient for us to feel the inspiration.

Calling to our sources of inspiration, feeling the energy, even if just a glimpse of it, we allow it to flow through us. This is our creativity, here manifesting itself as the craft of healing. Directing the inspired emotion into the physical, into the warmth of touch, of confidence, of love and support, soul to soul, spirit to spirit, we share the blessings, making a gift of what we have been given.

A good deal of healing is found simply by calling to the spirits of place, the trees and the wind, the land beneath our feet, the stream passing by, the grass and the birds, indeed all that makes up the web of energy, the colours and scents of creation immediately around us, above us, below us. Opening our eyes to the beauty of the world, to its growing and dying, its holding on and its free flight, its stability and fluidity, we see not only the mysteries of sacred nature which nourish so deeply but also the bigger picture beyond our own crisis.

A tree lives perhaps for 600 years, perhaps 1,500 or even longer, and our lives as human beings which cover a period of less than a century are a comparatively small part of their vision of the world. We run at such speed, clumsy and worried, tripping on the rocks and roots we've not had the time to see lying beneath our feet.

The rabbit that sits nonchalantly in the meadow at dawn is suddenly gone at the snap of a twig underfoot. The butterfly, utterly focused on her courtship dance, the bee laden with pollen, heavy in the sunshine, the fox following the scent that so saturates his mind – in the simplicity of our calling to those creatures around us, asking for guidance, making our offerings, we are shown different worlds, where pain and death are better understood, where the ebb and flow are more gracefully accepted.

Druidry is so much about the art of good relationship and the way in which we connect spirit to spirit. It is a tradition which is naturally healing, for healing has the same foundation.

DEEPENING RELATIONSHIP

Some momentary rituals are opportunities taken simply for the sake of deepening a relationship. No healing is needed, no change required. Our perception of the world as sacred now and then almost literally makes us pause, just to stop and soak up the energy. The Grail is overflowing.

Our thanks for these moments of delicious *awen* are given as offerings of our creativity. Yet we know that if our connection with the sources were deeper, if we were better attuned to the cycles and flows of nature, sharing intimacy with the courage to dive deeper into the mysteries, the *awen* would pour still more strongly through our souls.

It is for this reason that so much attention is given to the seasons and their festivals through the course of the year. They are the subject of our next chapter.

rituals for eight

FESTIVALS

THE IMPORTANCE OF THE FESTIVALS

When we think about the festivals of our ancestors, there is often a doubt that lingers in the minds of those first learning of the old traditions. What is the relevance of these holy days in a modern culture, with a new millennium stretching before us?

The simple answer lies in the source of Druidry: the fact that the tradition emerged out of a deep desire to connect with the powers of nature within us and around us. Despite all that our culture does to remove itself from the muddy wet unpredictability of the wild, we are still entirely dependent on the flow of nature, the tides of the ocean, the swirling currents of our weather systems, the fertility of the land, the compassion of the heart. Irritation and love, the comfort of home, the savour of good food, the rainy days and darkness of winter, the baked earth and fear of hunger, these issues still rule our lives as they ruled the lives of our ancestors. We can't tame the power of nature, we can only learn to co-operate with it. The harvest is still crucial to the well-being of our culture, whether we live in the big city or in the midst of the fields. There is a potency in remembering that.

By waking to the flows of the seasons we can better attune with their tides, so riding the surf instead of pulling against it. The more aware we are of the environment around us, the more in touch with the natural cycles, the closer we find ourselves to their rise and fall. We withdraw in the winter to the hearth circle of our tribe, feel the energy gently start to rise as the sun once more warms the earth in spring, as we open again in the summer, a vibrant flower, our leaves drinking in the sun until the petals fall and the fruit begins to swell, ripening, ready to drop back to the earth when autumn comes and again we will turn to gather up our lives, preparing for the darkness of winter. Living in tune with the seasons of our climate, finding a deeper connection, a congruence between our internal and our external environment, doesn't hold us back, but slows us to a more natural pace of life. Less energy is wasted. Empathy is easier, community stronger.

While our ancestors needed indicator points to guide them along the trackway of the year, allowing them to anticipate the movement of animals, the changing of the seasons, the most efficient times to sow and anticipate the harvest in a world without calendars, we may not need such primitive measuring sticks, yet the festivals are still potent markers for us. We may not *need* to know when the longest day has come, but without knowing it we lose an opportunity for magical inspiration. We may not be aware just when the moon is full, yet its gravitational pull affects us, emotionally, hormonally; in knowing the course of the lunar tide, we can use its energy beneficially instead of subconsciously fighting against it for the sake of stability. As the new corn grows rich and green in the fields, so we can nurture it within ourselves. As the crop is harvested, we too can assess the abundance and the value of what we have created, how we have invested, and as the fields are ploughed, revealing the dark earth beneath, we have the opportunity to turn over the earth within our own minds, within our own lives, preparing for a fresh new season to begin. With each dark moon, we can assess where we have come to, pruning off what is redundant and allowing the good fruit to grow round and sweet with the swelling moonlight.

The worlds around us offer us a constant flow of guiding currents, helping us to change and grow as we journey to find our joy and our fulfilment. Whereas the old festivals used to be an expression of the tribe's direct connection with the environment, affirming and celebrating the powers of light, fertility, abundance and death, so for many now living in urban IT environments they are rather more symbolic. The magical power in each celebration of the turning cycle of the year is about the psyche more than the land. However, it is important not to forget that the rituals are woven entirely with natural imagery and so act as a key reminder that all of us are still utterly dependent on Mother Nature.

THE TRADITION OF FESTIVAL RITUAL

The archaeological record gives us clear ideas about how important specific times in the year were to our ancestors. In days when darkness and cold were crippling, the need to reach out to those powers that gripped the land must have been profound. Asking for some sweet release, for the strength to make it through until the spring, for some understanding of the force that pushed so hard, our ancestors played out their need in ritual.

From the hunter-gatherer tribes of the Pretannic lands, over 5,000 years ago, there is evidence for rituals that clearly focused on the rebirth of the sun at midwinter. Working again with the tomb shrines, long barrows and passage graves holding the bones of our ancestors, it is possible to imagine an ancestral priesthood journeying back into the womb of the earth, dark and damp, a place of death and yet a source of new life.

As agriculture took root, the old nomadic tribes beginning to settle, claiming land and domesticating stock, the importance of the calendar grew. Of the shrines and temples that we have discovered, the standing stones and circles of the Bronze and Iron Age period, a more complex focus reveals alignments that indicate the marker days of the solstices and equinoxes. These were clearly used as guiding points for measuring the passing of the year.

What are now called 'the cross quarter days' are festivals that mark and celebrate the beginning of the four seasons of the agricultural year: winter, spring, summer and harvest. There is rich evidence of these festivals being celebrated by our ancestors in medieval literature, as well as in folklore. As seasonal changing points, they would most certainly have been celebrated for thousands of years into the past, though we've little knowledge of how.

We do know that our ancestors did not celebrate all the eight festivals now important to modern Druids and others in European Pagan traditions. Old texts and folk traditions tell us of some communities celebrating festivals with a rich exuberance, while other tribes make no mention of them. Why this might have been, we don't clearly know, but traditions do evolve within local culture, inspired by the native spirits, both those of the people and the land.

Druids of some 200 years ago were celebrating just the three solar festivals of the equinoxes and the summer solstice (though some say they honoured midwinter, but not in public ritual, owing to the cold).

It was Ross Nichols, a Druid in one of the old Orders, whose discoveries in the 1940s, made through exploring the medieval literature, inspired him to put together a 'wheel' of what he found to be eight perfectly spaced festivals throughout the year. Elders in his own Order were unimpressed and reticent to change what was established as their tradition, so Nichols took his ideas to Gerald Gardner, a friend and occultist who himself was in the process of reinventing a Pagan tradition of witchcraft he called Wicca. While Gardner happily took Nichols' idea into his development of Wicca, it took Nichols a little longer. His wheel of the ritual year was brought into Druidry when he left the old Druid Order to create his own group in the 1960s.

Through the spread of Wicca and Druidry over the past decades, the eight-festival year has spread across the world, influencing the development of many alternative, New Age and European Pagan spiritualities.

THE FORM AND PURPOSE

Although deeply fundamental changes can be achieved through careful and focused working with the festivals, the overwhelming reason for acknowledging the cycle is essentially that of celebration. In celebration, in the highs of its laughter and the current of its release, the potency of its sacred blessings, its abundance shared, profound connections of thanks and beauty are made within which there is healing beyond almost any other source. We find ourselves in the sacred gap between the past and the future, in a moment of time and space ... here and now ... and, pausing to watch, we can feel the exquisite energies of life as it moves humming through us.

Let the *awen* flow.

Samhain

The commonly used names for the cross quarter days are those in Irish Gaelic and I've used these as titles. There are alternative spellings, but in the main the first is pronounced *sow-in*, meaning 'summer's end'. It is also seen as Samhuinn in Scots Gaelic. Calan Gaeaf is the Welsh/British name for the festival, meaning 'the Calends of Winter', the eve being Nos Galan Gaeaf. Other names used are Ancestor Night and the Feast of the Dead. In Christian tradition it is known as Hallowe'en, and stretches through the mass days of All Saints and All Souls. By the written calender, the festival lies between 31 October and 2 November. Those who welcome the coming of winter by the changing weather, not the date, celebrate when the first frosts veil the ground.

THE RITUAL

The Spirits of Place are honoured and acceptance of our presence is requested. The Call for Peace is made. The *Nemeton* Circle is cast.

Because Calan Gaeaf is a ceremony that is about closure, about the darkness of winter creeping into our bones, infiltrating our many worlds, it is often especially important at this festival to secure the *nemeton* by casting the circle clearly, detaching it from the surrounding environment. In order to work with subjects that are fraught with taboos, tapping into the primary drive of survival, to feel a sense of safety the boundaries need to be strong.

To consecrate a rich earthy incense might be used, musky with dragon's blood, juniper berries and oil. The water might come from a iron-rich 'red' spring.

The Circle is consecrated with incense and water. The Quarters are honoured, their energies invited into the Circle. The Three Worlds are honoured.

The spirits of place at this time have their own character. The skies are often thick with tumbling clouds, the fields are ploughed over, the dark earth rough and naked. Those creatures who would are now disappearing into their dens of hibernation, the summer birds have gone south. There is a silence, when the winds are still. The seas are high, the waves crashing upon the shores of our lands, rain wets the air and fills the rivers. It is important that we tap into how this makes us feel, how we respond to the coming winter – for we do, intuitively and subconsciously, just as much as the badger, house martin and field mouse, though we fight it with central heating and electric lights. Feeling the changes within us, honouring them as we make our call to the spirits of place, is a major part of the value of this rite. Giving offerings to the spirits, setting out food for those creatures of the wild displaced by human dwellings, those perhaps disturbed by our Grove ceremony, affirming that we will fill the birdbath through the cold moons, all this can be done at this time in the rite, allowing all present to be involved, directly or indirectly.

Our ancestors are normally called at this point of a ritual, but because this is Calan Gaeaf, working with the ancestors is done as a key part of the ceremony a little later on.

The declaration of the purpose of the ritual is made, beginning with the welcoming to all in body and spirit, all those seen and unseen who have gathered within the intention of the circle. There is a few minutes' silence, a time when everyone can bring themselves into the sacred moment of here and now, letting go of the distractions of the outside world, focusing, committing to being present.

Welcome is offered to all present and presence is affirmed. Declaration and CHALLENGE: What is this time? Calan Gaeaf, a time of winter, darkness, death.

Here members of the Grove talk in poetry and drama, expressing what it is that the festival represents: a time of endings, the summer past, winter coming with its power of darkness. As my Grove is led by women, it tends to be focused on their experience, but it need not be so. In a Grove which is clearly based in male Druidry (most rituals that have evolved out of the eighteenth-century revival of the tradition are solar- and male-oriented) or one which works pro-actively within more of a balance, the questions and responses may be different. The important point is that what is expressed is of personal experience and, in a group or Grove, is generic for the whole within the nature of our local environment and climate.

At Calan Gaeaf, the harvest is all in, the deciduous trees are being stripped of their leaves, the last of summer's growth is being killed back by the icy fingers of frost. For our ancestors this was the beginning of several lean months. The livestock were brought into the winter pens and any that were too weak to last through the cold moons would be slaughtered, their meat prepared for storage, their blood and offal forming a large part of the Samhain feasting. Even now, we look to the frailest of our communities as winter looms, wondering if they will make it through. Though earliest records tell little about honouring the dead at this festival, it is clearly a time when the boundaries between the living and the dead are at their most blurred. It is a time of spirits drifting ...

Call to Ancestors, those of blood, heritage, the land; the veils are thin.

When we call to our ancestors, their names can be said aloud or in the silence of our souls. This is a time of mourning, of sadness openly expressed, and tears freely fall. In some rites a candle is lit for each soul whose name is spoken. In our culture to mention the names of the dead is an invocation, a 'call' that invites that soul to attend the rite, to share with us again. Some might do this in a way which is very direct, feeling a certainty that the souls of their loved ones do once again join them, standing by the fire. Others have no sense of this presence of folk from the 'otherworlds', but know that in saying the names the blessings and prayers of the ritual are directed towards them.

Ancestors of our blood, our teachers and those of our spiritual heritage, those of the land upon which we live and in which we celebrate the ritual, are all honoured and some may specifically be called.

CHALLENGE: What have we done with the past cycle, witnessed by the community, our families, our Ancestors?

In any ritual it is important to know where we are and where we have come from. Time can here be spent mulling over how we have spent the 12 moons since last Calan Gaeaf. Did we clear the old properly away, prepare the land well and sow seed which was of value? Did we nurture the seedlings, care for our crops, our soul creativity and our relationships? What did we harvest and how did we respond to the harvest we were able to take? We are naked before the spirits of our ancestors, our relationship spirit to spirit hiding nothing. It is a time of honesty, soul deep.

CHALLENGE: How will we go on into the cold moons? How will we best use our harvest, honouring self, community, guides, teachers?

Through the gluttony of our insecurity, the weight of the burden that is a lack of faith, it is easy for us to cling onto what we have. The drive that is our fear of change, which insists that familiarity is the best course, jeopardizes the value of what we have gained. In the Calan Gaeaf ritual we are given the opportunity to check what instinctively we want to hold onto, and consider whether it is wise or necessary. What is it we need take with us? What is redundant?

Call to Gods for guidance and to witness.

Now is the time to honour the gods, the powers of nature, of both the internal and external environments within which we live, our sources of inspiration. This can be done formally, by a member of the Grove making a respectful and ceremonial invocation, particularly if all those present are happy and willing to work with the same deities. In a ritual where those gathered honour different gods, the invocations may be to gods of the land (often unnamed gods of the mountain, the river, the soil and mist), as opposed to those of the ancestors, which are less often shared by a group (such as Odin, Rhiannon, Hecate, Jesus), or to generic deity forms such as Mother Earth and Father Sky ... Many may make the invocations, either aloud or silently within themselves. It is important that everyone present feels that they have an opportunity to call to their own source of power, beauty and inspiration, asking for guidance through the ritual and the cold moons to come.

Honour the Fire Spirits of transformation in the darkness. Release into the fire the dross, the masks we would let go.

Before releasing the unnecessary burdens we were in danger of carrying through the hardest part of the year, we honour the element which will work with us, ensuring that the release is final and powerful. To toss our rubbish into any element without first asking is disrespectful in the extreme.

In some rituals it is effective to have a member of the Grove dressed in the guise of the spirit of winter. She may represent a local form of the Cailleach, the wild hag, or he may be a white gleam of old Jack Frost. This spirit might scream and snarl, evoking and provoking the members of the Grove into thinking about their fears. The person plays the part of a kind of joker, hurling the mind into a new perspective, into honesty. She may carry with her a cauldron into which symbols of the redundant burdens are thrown by those in the circle. She might evoke laughter, or fear. She will provoke change.

Symbols of what is to be released are then given to the fire. Grove members might speak aloud what it is they release, or their words, affirmations, declarations, may be voiced internally. It is important that each person feels active in the process of release and empowered by witnessing their symbol being burned.

Symbols might be made of paper, with words written in ink, tears or menstrual blood. They may be of cloth, of twigs and grasses, dried flowers, whittled wood or food. They may be masks, created of papier maché or card, signifying a face we no longer wish to express. The creation must be inspired, emotion poured into it through the commitment (the very real desire) to let it go. As we watch these symbols burn, the emotion we have imbued them with resonates within us, dissolving into dust.

If another element is used – water, earth or air – the elemental spirits must be first honoured and the nature of the symbol that represents what is to be released must be soluble, biodegradable or dissipated, so that the element does indeed destroy and transform what is released.

Closing of the Year: Burning of the Spirit of the Year.

Samhain is the end of the year, a time of closure – an art little taught in our Western culture. The festival gives us an opportunity to work with this in many ways. Releasing the dross is the first. Then comes the actual declaration that the cycle is over. Gone.

This can be done simply by yelling into the wind! Alternatively, a more formal statement can be made. It is important, however, that it is done and that all gathered feel the effect. For this reason an effigy is often used, a 'Spirit of the Old Year' that can be burned upon the fire. Crafted of old straw, clematis and honeysuckle wood, ivy, dried flowers, herbs, seedheads of the season past, perhaps dressed in old clothes, the Spirit of the Year represents all that we put behind us, guiding us to make that difficult statement of letting go fully and honestly.

Although it is unlikely that the 5 November celebrations of burning the 'guy' would have become a part of our folklore without the reckless Guy Fawkes' attempt to blow up the king and parliament in 1605, this 'guy' has been the Pope (in Reformation England), the Devil and others. It is a perfect and potent way of exorcising the past.

Chaos comes, the Cailleach is welcomed and cacophony fills the air, taking us into the void.

Though the old year is over, the new is not begun, not in any way that is tangible. When the sun is reborn at Midwinter a new cycle will be ushered in, but until then there is the chaos of the dark, and this can be represented in the Grove. It is a time when life is upside-down, inside out and back to front. Modern Hallowe'en's trick o'treating is a fine expression of this and our ancestors too used trickery and deception, releasing the fear and crises of the time which is no time. Cross-dressing and stealing, joking and spilling danger all about, it was a festival of insanity.

Chaos, then, in this Grove rite is talked through in a wild drama of language and dance by the three women, as the Cailleach of winter is welcomed and slowly all those gathered take up their drums and rattles, whooping into the night, dancing, releasing their souls into the noise and disorder ... until naturally it dissolves into a tingling silence, the darkness of winter slipping in.

Darkness has become, through our monotheistic culture, an expression of evil. In Druidry it holds no such negative connotations. In darkness there is the power of the unknown. Darkness is the womb of the mother, the womb of all creation. So in this rite we are given the opportunity to reclaim the darkness and the value of decay, the mysterious power of death with all its crucial teachings. This can be done in many ways, honouring the value of the mud and humus that fertilizes our soil and feeds us. In this rite of my Grove, we honoured the native creatures that thrive in the darkness and feed off death.

Reclaim the right to find nourishment in decay. Hail owl, crow, badger, bat and mole, teachers of death and the power of night. Hail Ancestors, of old and those newly departed, Ancestors within, those in body, blood to blood, share in our feasting. Offerings to the Ancestors.

As in every ceremony, there is now a ritual feast of bread and mead, or similar. In the Calan Gaeaf rite, the bread is often black – fruitcake, rye bread or some other form. The mead may be replaced with a dark stout or port wine. The first part is offered in this rite to the ancestors, the next to the earth, and then it is shared around the circle.

In some rites of this festival the offerings made to the ancestors are of the 'four sacred foods' of Samhain – bread, honey, salt and wine. This can be done formally, with the powers of the four directions blessing the gifts before they are passed into the flames. It is my experience that many ancestors do appreciate a 'honey sandwich' and the purifying touch of salt with, of course, the libation of wine, beer or mead.

Affirm Circle of Community, support through the cold moons. *Awen*: Until the Sun is reborn, as we die let us be centred ... Prayers and affirmations.

Calan Gaeaf is the last time that folks are willing to travel far. For our ancestors, winter brought a pause to both trading and war. Community becomes more criti-

cal and in the rites of the festival the oaths we make of kinship and mutual support are important, spirit to spirit, human to human to tree to brook to bird to badger, to all of creation.

Sharing the *awen* chant, calling for inspiration, we request and affirm that the winter moons will be manageable. We assert that this time of chaos will be well used. Prayers are said so that the energy of the ritual may be shared, grounding our intentions, starting the process of returning our consciousness to the worlds beyond the bounds of the *nemeton*.

Thanks to Ancestors and the Gods. The Four Directions are honoured. The Circle is opened and the last Words of Peace given. The Spirits of Place are honoured.

So the Calan Gaeaf ritual ends ...

If the weather is fine, which is rather unusual, the feasting and *eisteddfod* can be shared outside in the ritual circle, by the fire. More often than not, by the end of a winter rite, when the protective barriers of the circle are lifted the cold floods in and folks are rather grateful to finish honouring the winter's arrival and get warm inside!

Food brought for the feast shared might be given a theme, as at any Hallowe'en party – red food to honour the blood, dark and black food to honour the night, and all kinds of 'spider' cakes and 'bone' pies to honour the dead, with laughter and respect. Jack o'lanterns made of pumpkins or squashes, marrows or turnips, signify the spirit of the old year, the light of the little candle sparkling out through the eye sockets, lighting the room, scaring 'evil' spirits from the window ledge or by the front door. These vegetable heads should be returned to the earth after the festival, buried in a compost heap to ensure a good new cycle ahead.

Midwinter

The festival of Midwinter begins with the ceremonies of the winter solstice, the shortest day of the year and the longest night, when the power of darkness is honoured, the divine mother, the womb of creation. This is a specific astronomical moment and occurs anywhere between 20 and 23 December. Three days later, between 23 and 26 December, it is possible, without technological help, to see along the horizon that the sun is rising once more nearer to the east. This is the more traditional time for celebration. So, although Druids don't celebrate Christmas, the winter rites are held on and around the same days.

Midwinter in the Druid tradition is called Alban Arthan, Welsh/Brythonic for 'the light of the bear'. For some it is understood to imply both the constellation of the Great Bear in our northern winter skies, and also Arthur, the saviour king and mythic hero of the British Isles. Historically a Christian Romano-British warrior king, Arthur fought the Pagan Saxons, delaying their incursions into the Pretannic Isles for two more generations.

While normally I would celebrate the festival in two rituals, here I will give it as one. It can easily be split, or ideas from the rite used as and when it seems appropriate.

THE RITUAL

The Alban Arthan rite might be held at dusk and begin with a fire being set in the centre of the circle but not yet lit. There may be darkness all around, cold and damp with winter's touch.

The Spirits of Place are honoured and acceptance of our presence is requested, the Call for Peace is made and the Circle is cast. The Circle is consecrated with incense and water. The Quarters are honoured, their energies invited into the Circle. The Three Worlds are honoured.

Alban Arthan is usually a quieter ceremony than Calan Gaeaf. As it is a ritual of family and close friends, the circle is often cast with the clear intention of it being an affirmation of the bonds of the community. If deep healing is to be done, if there is great fear of the dark or other issues to be dealt with, the casting should distinctly separate the circle from life outside the nemeton.

Incense for consecration might be enriched with orange peel, cinnamon and dried fruit. The nature of the three worlds, the spirits of place, are quite different from at Calan Gaeaf. Honouring the change is, again, one of the most potent parts of the ritual and an essential element even in the shortest observance.

When the ancestors are called in this rite, all gathered are given an opportunity to make offerings to the earth or air as inspiration or creativity. Gifts of food are made, of songs, seeds and intention. There is an understanding that the ease and teachings of the winter so far have been received and thanks are made to the ancestors. Their spirits will have been close through the darkening days.

The Ancestors are honoured; offerings of thanks are made. Welcome to all present. Presence is affirmed.

When the declaration of the rite is made, if this is on the solstice, the first eve of darkest winter, the statement of 'here and now' will be quite different from what is said on midwinter's eve or at the rite performed when the news of the sun's rebirth has been affirmed. Yet whether we are celebrating the power of darkness or the child reborn, the challenge takes us into understanding the night.

CHALLENGE: What is this time?
The longest night, Alban Arthan, the night of the bear. What is the power of darkness? What are the fears that now linger within us? The claws of unknowing, of annihilation, the void of the universe? What have we lost in the chaos? What do we mourn?

By understanding the power of darkness we are again reclaiming it as something which is useable instead of a source of threat that must be tamed with lights and knowledge. First we look to the fear. In the rite this might be dramatized by one or more members of the Grove, crone women who come weaving, screeching, 'What do you fear, mortal?', and lords of the hunt who gaze with pale death in their eyes. Those who play these roles are folk who would find release while intensifying their need to experience in sacred space the essence of this time. Their role is to frighten, to provoke and explore the realms of what is primally unsettling. At the same time, as with any drama, especially that done in sacred space, there is an element of wild inner laughter: we see the sweet childish vulnerability of our human souls, and that is magnified before the elemental and divine forces of nature. Obviously, if there are children in the gathering the level of fear is reduced appropriately.

Once we have found what it is we fear in darkness, it is time to look more deeply within and find the value of the dark, the potential of the void, the womb of creation. In Druidry it is clearly understood that where there is the greatest power and potential, there is also the greatest fear. So we might be given the opportunity in the Alban Arthan rite to see within the fear. In doing so we are again centring ourselves into the here and now, attuning with the cycle, bringing the internal into congruence with the external environment.

CHALLENGE: What would we do with it?
Dive into its clutches? Turn and walk away? Where is the power in this fear? What does it offer you?

Each soul gathered might speak aloud or allow the understanding to drift within. Though we may not grasp what the lesson truly is until later, the question will clarify the intention.

In the potential of darkness is the place of rebirth. Yet birth is a result of union and this is where the rite moves its focus now. The darkness is the womb, symbolized in Druidry by the cauldron or chalice, the Holy Grail. Conception requires the male principle too, represented by the sacred dagger, the wand or sword, Excalibur. To our ancestors, as for ourselves, divine union is exquisitely exemplified by that point when the shaft of star-sunlight touches the cervix and enters deep into the womb of the tomb shrine, reconsecrating and reinspiring the ancestors' bones, renewing life.

So in the ritual the symbols of male and female power are revered. This might be done in a number of different ways. The sacred knife and chalice might, in turn, be blessed and consecrated with incense and water, or with the four elements independently. They may then be offered to the service of the key god and goddess revered within the Grove. Generically this may be simply the sky father and earth mother, or the sun king and moon or ocean queen. Other symbols may be used as mentioned above.

The Male and Female Principles are consecrated and honoured.

Blessed and energized, the knife and cup might be taken around the Grove by the two who have performed the consecration, or replaced on the altar so that every member might make his own act of reverence, saying a prayer, giving a word of dedication or loyalty, making an offering.

The Rite of the Mistletoe is performed, the bough held high by the priest in the south. The priestess in the north walks to the centre, where the blessings are made over the unlit fire. The gathering is asked, 'What would you have of this union? What do you wish to be conceived?' The *Awen* is called, each soul reaching for the power of inspiration, its flow moving through us. The bough is grounded.

Mistletoe is a herb most sacred in the tradition. It is mentioned in the oldest texts that Druids in France used to collect it and work with it in a highly sacred manner. It was said to have extraordinarily powerful and magical qualities.

In the ritual, the priestess walks from the north, the place of womb darkness, as the priest walks from the south, the place of light. He holds the bough that represents his male fertility; the white berries are filled with a liquid that closely resembles sperm. Yet mistletoe is a plant that grows high on the branches of other trees, never rooting in the earth, taking its nourishment from the tree on which it dwells, and it is therefore considered to be a plant of the sky gods, sacred to the sun. It is understood that it retains its magical power of fertility only if it has never touched the ground, at which point the power 'spills' as if the sperm were ejaculated.

When the Druids come together in the centre of the circle, the priest holds the bough out over the unlit fire so that the two, male and female, touch its stems, its leaves and berries. He calls to his lord of the skies, asking that the herb be blessed, as the priestess calls to her lady of the dark earth, asking for blessings upon it too, charging it with divine energy. Those gathered are then given the opportunity to work with the couple, infusing the process with their own desires for the union. What would each soul wish to birth anew? The chant of *awen* strengthens our resolve to be guided, inspired, to understand what it is we desire. When the group's focus is taut, the Druid priest and priestess together slowly bring the bough down to the earth, so that the sky lord's fertility might spill into the womb of earth.

Lightning, another gift of the sky gods' power, is understood to have been the force which activated life on Earth in the beginning of time. Magically, symbolically, mistletoe is said to have the same effect.

The Mistletoe is shared with blessings.

The bough is then broken into as many pieces as are needed, each sprig containing a leaf pair and berry or berries, so that the gift of divine fertility can be shared with all those gathered for the ritual. Holding within it the sacred lore of immortality, the mistletoe is known as all-heal, and each Grove member can use the sprig as a blessing on their house and hearth, their work and creativity, throughout the cycle that is about to be born.

The rite so far has been carried out in as much darkness as is feasible. Only one lantern has been alight and that has been veiled. It is now lifted in its place, at the point where the midwinter sun will rise: the south east. On the wheel of festivals, this is the point of Beltane, the festival of love, and in this Midwinter rite the lantern might be raised with a pale yellow rose.

In the place of love, the lantern is unveiled. The light shines out, tender and new, and the birth of a new sun is declared, a tiny light, the *Mabon* Child reborn. All 'Hail and Welcome' the sun, still wrapped in the dark robes of his Mother Earth.

The 'Hail and Welcome!' might be wild celebration or a more formal statement, depending on the nature of the gathering. Specific deities of sun might here be invoked and revered, poetry spoken, songs of welcome sung and music played that

would honour both the mother and the infant light. As the celebration grows, each soul gathered might lay an offering with the rose at the lantern side.

All lanterns are lit from the one lantern.

So it is that the light is shared. This light (or the spirit of this light if the candles are extinguished and relit at a later time) is a reminder and a focus for all who have been at the ritual celebration of the inner light reborn. Through the slow and dreary days of Capricorn, when the sun is still a gentle child, not strong enough yet to offer us warmth, this light is a memory of the greater light in the sacred fire and in the sun that will grow, bringing us summer's heat.

When the lanterns are all burning, the main fire is lit from the original flame.

The fire is lit with celebration! Prayers are said within the power of this energy.

As with each rite, prayers are a part of the integration process, allowing the power of the ritual, with all its changes, to seep through our subconscious, finding direction, so that when the circle is opened the energy will flow appropriately. Our prayers are focused on ourselves, our community and our world as a whole. They may be said aloud or within our own souls.

The ritual Feasting and *Eisteddfod*.

The bread and mead are blessed, the first part offered to the earth, the mother who has birthed the sun, the second to the *mabon* (Welsh for child) in the sacred fire, before the rest is shared around the circle. If the fire is strong and the weather bearable, the feasting may continue with stories and poems, tales of winter. If it is just too cold, snowy or wet, the feasting and *eisteddfod* will continue indoors around the hearth, after the rite is over.

Thanks are given to Ancestors and Gods, the Quarters are honoured, the Circle is opened and the last Words of Peace given. The Spirits of Place are honoured.

And the Midwinter rite ends ...

Alban Arthan is then a turning-point within the season winter. It marks the change from the chaos that is not knowing, the pain of labour that is the swirling hurricane within the cauldron of rebirth, to the slow silence of life just after the birth. There is serenity and pain in healing. There is anticipation, yet precious stillness.

Traditionally, evergreen boughs of ivy and holly are brought indoors to affirm the power of life renewed. Using special wood for the fire is also traditional, the oak log or Yule log being one great piece of wood which was burned over the course of 12 days until Twelfth night. Bundles of ash sticks were burned on Midwinter's day, serving the same purpose of both offering blessings of abundance and protecting the house from negative entities. The 12 days are representative of the 12 months to come and divination is often used through this period to determine the course of the coming year. After 6 January, the ploughing season began for our medieval ancestral farmers.

The Midwinter feast is rich with abundance, traditionally following a period of restraint, with plum puddings and cakes, made dark with dried fruit, and a trinket or coin hidden within serving as a lucky omen. Presents are shared to hold the community and family together through the coldest part of winter, which is yet to come.

Imbolc

This is the festival that celebrates the beginning of spring, the first signs of life now beginning to emerge. Also spelled Imbolg, pronounced *im-olk*, or Oimelc in Gaelic, it is often known as Brighid's Day. In Welsh, it is Gwyl Forwyn, pronounced *gwil vor-wun*, the feast of the maiden, or Gwyl Fair, the feast of Mary, Brighid having the role equivalent to Mary, the divine mother, in pre-Christian Britain. Unlike Mary the perpetual virgin, however, Brighid evolves through the cycles of woman, and at this rite she is felt in her triplicity, as mother reflecting in the innocence of her child, as hag in the darkness of the womb's blood and ploughed earth. Candlemas is the same rite within the Christian tradition. Celebrated by the calendar between 1 and 2 February, for those who go by the seasons the festival comes when the first snowdrops are flowering, the first lambs are born or when the energy of the Earth can first truly be felt stirring. It is a festival which celebrates the mother who has given birth, the magical beauty of the *mabon* and all new life.

THE RITUAL

While it is hard for many to perform a rite outside when the weather is so cold, in the tradition our festivals of the year are about celebrating the turning cycle, its rain and frost, its heat and draught. At Gwyl Forwyn, a fire might be deemed essential in order to prevent those who have gathered losing focus simply by freezing. However, this ritual isn't about the warmth of sunlight or about the heat of the fire: it is about the growing light in its infant tenderness, still held within the arms of the mother. If it is possible, then, a centre fire might be replaced with candles. Three or nine, representing sacred triplicity, might be lit and set in a cauldron or bowl of either earth or water, both symbolic of the womb.

As a festival, Gwyl Forwyn is usually one of the gentlest, quietest of rites, and few travel far to attend the gatherings, most preferring to stay within the warmth of family and local community.

The ritual begins as the others have, with the spirits of place being asked whether they will accept the presence of the gathering. The call for peace is made and the circle is cast, perhaps with a mist of white light, adding to the mystery of this festival of the power of dreams and potential.

The *nemeton* is consecrated with a soft incense, sweetened perhaps with myrrh and mullein, sandalwood and motherwort. The water might be of melted frost or snow. The four directions are honoured, the spirits of place from land, sea and sky, and the circle is complete.

When all present have been welcomed, a few minutes' silence is offered so that everyone gathered might come to know where they are, here and now, and for what intention, casting aside all distractions. Then the declaration of the rite is made.

CHALLENGE: What is this time?

At Calan Gaeaf we met, closing the year, the energy of chaos breaking around and within us. On Mother Night, the Winter Solstice, we honoured the power of the dark, and at Alban Arthan our celebrations of rebirth filled the air with light once more. Where have we come to now?

The sun is to us still a child, tender and vulnerable. We have walked through the last weeks since his birth with no lantern to guide us, reaching out to know the boundaries, to find some points of reference. We've been flailing around in the dark. Sensing our own vulnerability, we affirm the circle by holding hands and strengthen the group further by invoking the ancestors to join the rite.

Affirm Circle of Community, make the call to the Ancestors, teachers, parents, guides of blood, heritage and the land, asking for their blessings of protection, guidance and inspiration. Offerings are given both to the Ancestors and to the Spirits of Winter.

Though taking place in the depths of the cold, this rite affirms the beginning of spring. From what little we have, we make a sacrifice, a gift given with thanks to the ancestors for their guidance through the cold and dark moons so far and to the spirits of winter. In honouring the spirits of winter we are acknowledging what they have offered us, what the season has brought to us, taught us and freed from us. For though we may have been sheltered by our civilized society through the winter months, within us our reserves of light and warmth are low (what else is running low now?), and in giving of our meagre stores we assert our faith that we will again create abundance with the coming cycle of growth.

CHALLENGE: Time of dreams, a time of not knowing. The light is a child, hidden in his mother's robes, the light is a dream, hold the light-dream close ... Yet only the child dreams fully and openly, uninhibited, let us feel the child within us, dreaming, dreaming, free and unchained ... And we are the child, the child of our dreams, the child in our dreams, we are the light, tiny growing spark, hiding within the dark of our mother's robes ... What is your Fear, so small, so young, a light in the dark, vulnerable, unknowing? How tiny and vulnerable is the glinting light of your dreams?

In this rite of Gwyl Forwyn, we have the opportunity to feel ourselves as the mother who holds us and as the child who craves holding. While the child is symbolic of the sun, he also represents the seed-child of our new cycle of growth, that seed not yet ready to be sown in the cold earth but held as a dream, a hope, a potentiality.

One of the Grove might take the role of the mother goddess, drawing a sense of safety out of those gathered, evoking the feelings of the child. Another might take the role of the young sun-child, the seed-dream, inspiring in the circle parental feelings of nurturing and protection. To bring in a powerful male figure that would balance the rite's energy, if that were desired. So a star god, a high lord of light, a father of the sun might enter the rite, speaking of the qualities he would bring to such a time, his invulnerability and protection, another parent beside the Mother Earth.

The Mother Goddess holds, the Father God encourages, the Sun Child stretches, waking. The Circle honours the *Mabon* with blessings of song and poetry.

If the weather is fine enough, each soul might make an offering of creativity and respect to the mabon, otherwise a person might sing a song of reverence or recite a poem that is in keeping. In some rites, this might be formal, a dignified affair, whilst other Groves might play, finding strength in the spirit's light, freedom in the child's growth and awaking, evoking laughter with the poetry or stories told. There is power, joy and healing in the ability to reach into the free child within us. Respect, reverence, spirit to spirit connection and soul empowerment are what is important here, however ceremonially or informally that is achieved.

The *Awen* is called, followed by a call again to the Ancestors and Spirits of Place to clarify our dreams, then Brighid's Invocation. The candles are charged with the power of dreams.

Brighid, divine mother, is a goddess of inspiration and light. Some see her as white with purity, holding her power with a virgin's integrity. Others see her as earth-black and blood-red with strength, or brilliant with the golden flames of the candle's light, the fire's dance, the furnace's rage.

If Brighid is a deity that is honoured within the group she might be invoked here, but if this is not the case, another mother goddess or local deity of inspiration might be called, or the call to the gods may be left as a generic invocation.

The awen chant beforehand opens the rite to the flow of creative life energy. We call to our ancestors and to the spirits of place as we quest our inspiration, knowing that what we crave will affect all those around us in our internal and external environment. It is important that we clarify our dreams, our hopes and desires, forming them not from will but from divine vision, through responsibility and connectedness.

Each person will have brought candles with them to the rite. They are new and usually but not necessarily white. Holding the candle with full awareness, we pour into its form the imagery and emotion that are the dreams we hold for the coming cycle of growth. Our candles might be lit there in the ritual, from the candles already lit, and placed in the water or earth of the mother goddess. If this is not appropriate or easy to do, they might be brought back to the feasting place and lit there from those candles dedicated to the goddess and her mabon, the dream-prayers filling the room with individual dancing flames.

It will be a while yet before the earth is soft, warm, receptive enough for the sowing of seeds. Working here with our dreams allows us inspiration for patience. Seeds cast too soon will come to nothing.

Honour the Spirits of Fire that will burn the candles, asking that they be wise as they take our dreams into essence so that they might manifest, growing with the warmth of the sun upon our lands.

In the Ritual Feast the bread and mead are blessed and shared in a sacred manner. Thanks are given for the new life of those children born during the past 12 moons, their names are said aloud and blessings offered. Prayers of peace and healing are made.

Thanks are given to Ancestors and Gods, the Four Directions are honoured, the Circle is opened and the last Words of Peace given. The Spirits of Place are honoured.

The Gwyl Forwyn rite ends here ...

A wonderful custom not included in this rite is that of the white serpent. This magical creature of folklore is a representation perhaps of the earth energy emerging, the sap of spring waking. It is an earth 'dragon' that holds the energy of the land. Not wishing to deter the snake from its course, yet also perhaps wishing to appease its waking temper, offerings can be made to it, usually of milk.

The Gwyl Forwyn feast might have a theme of white foods, 'nursery' foods that soothe the child within us and dairy products for those that eat animal milk. The *eisteddfod* can be rich with songs, stories and poetry that focus on parenting and childhood issues.

The Spring Equinox

The Welsh/Brythonic name for this festival is Alban Eilir, meaning 'the light of spring', and it is the turning-point within the season of Imbolc, marking the time of equal night and day when the sun rises in the east. By the calendar it is at a specific point around 21–22 March and a great many of its traditions have been taken on by the Christian Church and blended into Easter, a word that itself stems from the Saxon goddess Eostra, having the same root as oestrus and oestrogen. It is a festival of fertility waking. From here on the days become longer than the nights.

The young sun god is taking up his weapons of manhood; the maiden of earth is shedding blood for the first time, moving forward through puberty, coy in her beauty, dressed in the golden flowers of springtime and sparkling rain.

THE RITUAL

The rite begins in the same way as the others have, calling to the spirits of place, affirming there is peace, casting the circle. In a ritual where there are children present

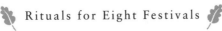

and the *nemeton* need not be so distinctly set, the casting may be done with the scattering of seeds and flowers. (When seeds are scattered, care should be taken that none will germinate unless they are native and non-invasive.)

The circle is consecrated with a light incense and clean rainwater. The four directions are honoured, as are the spirits of place that dwell in the three worlds. The ancestors are welcomed into the circle and the rite's intention is declared. It is affirmed that all who have come are present and focused.

CHALLENGE: What is this time?
A time of balance, a turning of the season and the year, the rite declared. The balance is struck ...

... meaning that a play is made between people in the circle, man and woman, parent and child, priest and priestess, calling words that counter each other such as 'Winter!' 'Summer!', 'Dark!' 'Light!', 'Woman!' 'Man!', 'Dying!' 'Growing!', 'Black!' 'White!', 'Death!' 'Life!' The play can be as formal or dramatic, as playful or explicit as is comfortable or appropriate for the company present. It might be filled with laughter or drawn into fuller lines that offer more than the simple words, ideas that are stated, accepted, challenged, overlaid, confronted and dismissed, as the gathering is drawn into a deeper understanding of time and place, of the festival itself. The celebration and the confusion, the perfection of balance is here, yet there is also the struggle of duality.

Honour the Spirits of Winter darkness, now behind us. The dark fertile earth of our sacred land is honoured, the womb of the new cycle. The soil is blessed and shared amongst those gathered.

Every soul present is invited to take a handful or is given a parcel of the consecrated soil. At this time prayers or blessings are spoken. The people gathered might speak of the beauty and power of their winter, of the lessons of the darkness, their experience of the birthing process. Just stating single words such as 'courage', 'family', 'cohesion' is a way of guiding folk to encapsulate what they have experienced, so clarifying and better owning the growth and understanding.

Ritual

As with every ritual, the focus within is a reflection of our attitudes to what is living around us. The internal is a constant mirror for the external and vice versa. So in making an offering to the spirit of winter, those spirits that thrive and are nourished in the darkness of night, the caves of our reality, we are also honouring what exists within our own dark inner world, acknowledging not only our inner strength but also all that lurks and hides in the cracks, unsure or unaccepted by our consciousness, too shy to be expressed.

As the festival is of the turning-point, we then turn to the light. This might be done by words, or more dramatically, with the altar to the winter in the north or north east, and that to the summer in the south or south east.

Honour the Spirits of Summer's light, shining ahead of us, all that is external, expressed and manifest. The young sun deity's growing warmth and light are honoured, offerings are made. Seeds are blessed and shared amongst those gathered.

How do we change from winter to summer? What is the transformatory process as we come to express what has been held within us?

At this time in the rite, honouring ourselves in the sun's light, open and free, stretching to grow, we make offerings to the fire that symbolizes the growing sun, offerings that express our hopes and growing clarity. Seeds are blessed and each person in the Grove is given a share in a little packet or pouch. These may be organic wheat or barley grain which, even if planted in a pot on the kitchen windowsill, will sprout and grow ripe in time for the harvest rites. Sunflowers or nasturtiums, beans or sweetpeas, or any beautiful annual grass or flower might be used. It is useful to bear in mind that many folk don't have particularly 'green' fingers, though, and choosing an easily grown hardy plant avoids stress and heartache ...

The consecrated soil is added to the soil in which the seeds are later sown.

In a more complex rite, instead of just soil and seeds, once the spirits of winter and those of summer have been honoured, each member of the Grove might take their own pot or container and walk to the north, there to be given earth to fill the pot, which is then blessed by the priestess. Moving to the east, a Grove member can be given seeds to be sown into the soil and a blessing be given. In the south, a priest can bless the sown seeds with the soft warmth of sunshine. In the west, consecrated rainwater can be sprinkled as a blessing upon the soil.

The Call is made to the Spirits of Summer to prepare for our coming. We find the balance point of now, the chant made *MA* to *AWEN*, the Spring Maiden and young Sun Lord taking their places.

Calling summer to be ready for us, we affirm that the seeds we have now sown or are soon to sow will be well received, germinating in the warm earth, blessed by the sun. Yet we must be patient. This is a time when fertility is just waking. We must return our focus to the point of balance in order to ensure the germination is strong and complete.

Instead of simply chanting the *awen* for inspiration, at this rite we might begin with a different sound, a '*mmmmaaaaaa*' sound that honours the sacred mother, the maiden who is warming to the touch of the sun. Facing inwards in the circle, we chant the '*ma*', allowing our voices to weave together, harmonizing and diving through each other's visions and emotions. As the chant changes into the *awen*, those in the circle turn gently to face outwards. Instead of inner and outer, the change may be north then south, or west then east. The young woman in the group who is to represent the spring maiden remains facing the way of the '*ma*' chant.

In the energy of the *Awen*, Prayers are said for the light growing, the spring sowing, the power of duality shared. All turn to the Maiden of Spring who walks to the centre of the Circle in the east. Any who wish come forward to give offerings and be blessed by her.

The spring maid of any Alban Eilir rite is a wonderful role to play. Adorned with a crown of flowers, dressed beautifully, innocently, for this special occasion, she is often the youngest woman of the gathering. Of all those who attend the rite, its impact is likely to be strongest on her life.

Any who wish can take their gifts and offerings to the maiden. Some she will accept, some she will bless and return. Painted eggs, holding the creativity and

emotion, the desires of a new growing season, seed-thoughts and plans, are offered to her. The bunnies and chicks of the Christian Easter are all a part of this same symbology: new life is offered so that the year may bring abundance. It is not always symbolic, though. A portion of the seeds that are to sown in our gardens, our allotments and the fields of our lands are also brought to the spring maiden to be blessed by her magical touch.

The last to come to her is the young sun lord.

The young Sun Lord gives his gift, his heart and his hand to her to dance.

Often the youngest fellow of the gathering, the sun lord is strong and free in his naïveté. He offers her his gift, his sweet soft spring light, perhaps in the form of the golden daffodils that glow with sunshine. He kisses her hand, with innocence and gentleness, and they dance in the circle. This dance may be accompanied by the harp or flute, played by any competent Bard of the Grove, or it may be to the more informal sound of the drums and feet stamping, the gathering cheering the young couple's self-conscious steps. There is no sexuality in this, no innuendo, simply the beauty of young love, first recognition, not yet sufficiently grown to be consummated. It is perfect balance, softly dancing its freedom, its tender learning, its new reality.

At the equinox, equal night and day is shared across the world, and as such it is a perfect time for affirming harmony and tolerance. When the dance is done and the couple rejoin the circle, prayers can be made, sharing the beauty and positive energy of the rite across the world, declaring through the intention that when the circle is opened its blessings of love, fertility and laughter should flow through the threads of spirit connectedness.

The Bread and Mead are blessed by the Spring Maiden and young Sun Lord, who give the first part to the land and the second to the sun-fire and the Ancestors before offering it to each other and sharing it, with blessings, amongst all those gathered.

Once the ritual feast has been shared, any last prayers or dedications are made within the sacred *nemeton* before the rite is closed. As with any rite, the feast and *eisteddfod* might be enjoyed within the ritual space if the weather allows.

Thanks are given to Ancestors and Gods, the Four Directions are honoured, the Circle is opened and the last Words of Peace are given. The Spirits of Place are honoured.

And the rite here ends ...

The underlying anticipation of summer is the energy that infuses the Alban Eilir ritual, a childish excitement that allows us the courage to take risks, to leap where winter's caution would have had us pause. The sap is rising and, taking time to listen, leaning up against a tree, it is possible to feel the energy of that extraordinary flow. As the sun's light warms the earth, we are provoked into stretching, reaching for the skies, eager to grow and learn, to find our freedom in new directions.

Beltane

This Irish Gaelic word, also spelled Belteinne or Bealteine, or in Scots Gaelic Bealtuinn, means 'bright or good fire' or 'fire of Bel', the old sun god whom Classical writers considered the same as their Apollo. In Welsh, it is Calan Mai, 'the Calends of May', and to those working by the calendar it is celebrated on 1 May. As Calan Mai is not deemed truly with us until the May tree or hawthorn has flowered, the rites may be adjusted to tie in with the opening of those sacred and beautiful white-pink blossoms.

Calan Mai is the festival that marks the beginning of summer. Wrapped in a great deal of delicious and easily found folklore, it is a festival as popular as Calan Gaeaf, marking the other side of the year and exploring the other deep human drive that is fraught with taboos: sex. While at Alban Eilir the young couple's love was platonic, by Beltane they have grown to know the pleasures of sexuality. The festival is one which celebrates union.

THE RITUAL

Traditionally at Calan Mai there is not one but two fires in the centre of the circle. A maypole may also be erected with ribbons of red and green, white and gold, or many colours. The altar is heavy with flowers, red roses and May blossom. Though some remove the thorns, most consider the risk of being pierced an important part in any ritual of love ...

The rite begins as any other. Because Calan Mai tends to be a ritual that is filled with dancing and revelry, the circle is seldom cast too firmly. If deeper transformation and healing are to be undertaken, then some of the rite here will serve only sketchily as ideas. Parts can be taken and others discarded. The importance of the rite is to honour the power of duality, attraction and rejection, give and take, push and pull.

As Druidry is a spirituality that works with relationships spirit to spirit, physical gender is not an issue. Where there is duality, this is understood to be both an internal and external relationship, regardless of biological or social gender identity.

The circle is consecrated with a musky incense, potent with damiana or some such aphrodisiac herb; the water used might be from a sacred spring or be dew collected before dawn (this is said to have great beautifying powers). The spirits of the four quarters and the three worlds are honoured, with a clear focus on how these have changed as our environment has been sliding into the warmth of summer. When the priestess is sure that there is focus and presence, the intention of the ritual is declared.

CHALLENGE: What is this time?
Calan Mai with hawthorn flowers, the beginning of summer, the fertility of the land, is brimming, the sap still rising fast, the leaves opening, the flowers offering nectar to the waking bees. It is time to honour sexuality, the powers of creativity.

Wherever we are dealing with sexuality, we are close to death, for within the power of sex is the potential for birth. By invoking life, we walk a path that is shadowed by death. By invoking pleasure, we walk a path that is tinged with pain. With every climax we surrender, diving through that arching wave of dying, a wave that will crash upon us with its flood of release.

As we call to the ancestors in this rite, we are doing so from the shadow of summer's light. Because this Grove is led by women, its focus is on the hag, but the Lord of the Hunt may as easily be invoked, or indeed both spirits/deities.

Call to the Ancestors.
CHALLENGE: Where is the hag?
She is within you, within your blood, in the darkness of your inside world. All are given gifts of winter, mud and naked honesty. She bows to the Maiden of Spring.

At Imbolc, the Cailleach of the wild mountains, the hag of winter, transforms into the maiden, the Forwyn of the spring. The Maiden speaks of this, then makes her own challenge, guiding those present to find their 'here and now'.

CHALLENGE: What have you sown?
The Spring Maiden is beautiful, young and free, sharing with the gathering her youthful energy and pure immortal optimism. All are given (or showered with) gifts of petals, seeds and hope. The Maiden then bows to the veiled May Queen and kneels beside her.

The Maiden does not nourish, she offers only beauty and potential. When the May Queen steps forward, her face covered, she offers herself as the Mother, Rhiannon, goddess of the land. But first she needs a lover ... In this rite, the Maiden kneels by her and the Hag calls to the men of the gathering.

CHALLENGING the men: who would face me and gain sovereignty of this land? Prove your value, strength and potency! Offer us your inspiration anew! The Sky Lord replies, taking with him those who would go to prepare the Maypole.

The Maypole, an obvious symbol of phallic power, is wrapped in the tangled dance of the last cycle's romancing. To drums and clapping, fiddles or flutes, the men dance their unravelling, unwinding the coloured ribbons. It's a time of laughter and honesty, clumsiness and camaraderie, a complicated business at the best of times! When they are done, the Maypole stands clean, the ribbons fluttering freely in the breeze.

Men and women separate, women within and men on the outside.

The Hag calls with words such as, 'Now get you gone from our circle, for we must feel who we are, of the earth and the moon, the womb of creation, finding true our sources of life alone!' And her partner, the Sky Lord, replies, 'Be sure we will be gone, for we must know our own power, our strength untouched by your wanting gaze!'

The women might stay in the centre, looking outwards, holding hands, the men silently circling, thinking, watching, waiting. The importance of the moment is the dance of duality, the up and down, day and night, warrior and lover, freedom and dependence. The paradoxes of life are addressed in this moment. If this needs to be clarified with words then it can be, in song or music, in a Bard's tale told or priest's understanding. Is there ever a possibility of merging, of real union?

The women talk, deciding, choosing, wondering what to do. 'Do we want them? Do we need them?' Chanting for inspiration, their voices are joined by those of the men.

The *Awen* is called, reaching for sources of inspiration to learn the pattern of the weave. Music and/or drumming guides the women to start to dance and the Maypole ribbons are woven.

The music that supports the women's dance around the Maypole can be of any kind. Traditional folk music with fiddles, flutes and bodhran, or the deeper sounds of purely drums and percussion, chanting and singing, or the dignity of the harp, all provoke a different kind of dance, formal and choreographed or chaotic and splashed with puddles of wild laughter. The women weave their dreams and desires of love and creativity, ducking and reaching over each other, ducking and reaching, twirling the coloured ribbons around the phallic pole, the tree of life, inspiring the land and the men who watch, driving the rhythm.

The May King walks forward to claim the May Queen from the weaving and they dance together within the Circle.

The May King is thought to represent many different aspects of nature or deity. He may be the sun god born at Alban Arthan, or the chieftain of the people who would wed the goddess of the land to bond a relationship that will bring him riches of abundance. He may be the vegetation god, the Corn God sown at Alban Eilir who will be slain at the harvest, or a horned god of the wildwood, Jack in the Green. Whomever we see him to be, it is his union with the May Queen, goddess of the land, that brings us the abundance we pray for.

Their dance ends before the Hag of Winter and the Sky Lord or Lord of the Hunt.

The Rite of Union honours the two coming together. Offerings are made by those gathered for the rite and the May couple give their blessings in return.

Quite often at Calan Mai, the May king and queen are a real couple and, at this point, the priest or priestess will act as celebrant for them in a real handfasting or Druid wedding or rededication of their marriage vows. (Such rites are explored in the next chapter.) If they are not a couple or don't wish to be wed, the 'Rite of Union' is an acknowledgement by those gathered that the two powers have joined. Everyone present has the opportunity to make offerings of gifts to the couple, who now represent a sacred and divine joining. They are, in return, given blessings of fertility and creativity.

The May couple first, then all present make their dance through the magical and cleansing Fires of Fertility.

Aloud or silently within the soul, any dedications, vows or prayers are made, and all who have gathered for the rite are given the opportunity to make their dance between or over the two fires of Calan Mai. The May couple go first to bless the path. Others may go through together, as couples, hand in hand. Some need to dance alone, taking with them their own special dreams of fertility and creativity, holding the inspiration of the rite and the blessings of the gods as they make their leap of faith.

Our ancestors used to drive their livestock between the two Beltane fires as a prayer of cleansing before taking them out into the summer pastures. The fires were said to drive away 'evil' spirits and bring fertility, new lovers, protection and prosperity.

The May couple bless and share the ritual feast of Bread and Mead, honouring absent friends, lovers old and new, and those loved ones who have now died. *Eisteddfod*. The Vow of Kinship is spoken.

With the last prayers, the ritual is closed in the normal way, honouring and giving thanks to the ancestors, the gods and the spirits of place with the four directions. Peace is affirmed and the circle is opened. So the rite ends ...

Calan Mai is a time of tree dressing: tying prayers, ribbons and strips of cloth onto the branches of sacred trees. It is a time of music and dancing, of courage and exuberant expression, of love and friendship. A celebration of creativity and sexuality, its greatest value perhaps is in the way such a ritual can break up taboos, fears and self-negations about our personal ability and worth.

Midsummer

As with the festival that marks the mid point of winter, so the festival of midsummer is also divided into two. We begin with the celebrations of the summer solstice, which is at some specific point between 20 and 23 June. It takes three days here, too, before we can be certain simply by watching the horizon that the year has turned on its axis and the sun is rising further towards the east once more. This brings us to what is known as Midsummer's Day, between 23 and 26 June (usually thought of as 24 June). In the Welsh/Brythonic it is called Alban Hefin, meaning 'light of summer'. In the Christian tradition, it is St John's Day and is especially important in some gnostic and mystic limbs of the faith.

The more we celebrate the changing cycle of nature through the year, the more we are able to connect deeply with it, finding a true congruence between the internal and external. I'm not sure it would be entirely sound for me not to add a note of caution at this point, for the solar tide does indeed rise and fall within us. It is impossible to generalize about how this affects us, for we each respond in different ways. While I simply adore the rites of Midwinter, allowing myself to slide further and further into the velvet embrace of the dark goddess, others find the time claustrophobic in the extreme, grabbing any excuse to snarl and scratch as their soul aches for the moment when fresh air and new light will touch their skin, offering once more the taste of freedom.

Midsummer is my nightmare. This is the time of the sun's greatest height, when its golden disk breaks the horizon at its furthest point north east, leaving the Pretannic Isles but four hours of twilight to claim as night. It is a time of open expression, of strength and assertion, of grandiose speeches made upon old hills and soap boxes. Politics is at its most self-righteous and pompous. It is a time of summer madness, the peak period between 20 and 23 June being the worst time, and if you don't wish to stay home under the sofa I declare it is a time fit only for celebration, wild carnival and sweet deep friendship. As the sun king stands tall in his moment of victory, blinkered with pride, he forgets that he is not invulnerable ... Then the spirits of the darkness begin silently to pull the carpet from underneath his feet. The tide has turned.

As with every festival, the most important issue here is how we feel at this time, what it is we sense a need to do. What is the landscape teaching us about its response to the weather, to the shifting patterns of light and dark, the changing energy?

THE RITUAL

As with Midwinter's rite I have given here just one ritual, the blending of a solstice and the release of Midsummer. I have not given the dawn rite, though very often a ritual is performed to welcome the rising sun, or a group gathers in silence to acknowledge the event. The ideas given here can be put into a dawn ceremony or used for ritual at any other time.

Because of the madness that so often surrounds the period, with all free expression and self-centred strength, the Midsummer rituals of my Grove are often an affirmation of acceptance and the power of friendship, family and community that balance the assertive fist of individuality. If we can perceive Midwinter as a time of close connection, Midsummer is its antithesis, declaring the virility of independence.

The rite begins as any other, by asking the spirits of place for acceptance and calling for peace. The *nemeton* circle is cast according to how separate the Grove feels it needs to be. As we call to the ancestors we ask respectfully for teaching.

CHALLENGE: What is this time?
Wild luscious growth, excess and progress, greatest over the powers of darkness, wild adventure and gleaming swords. The three gifts of inspiration are proclaimed.

At Gwyl Forwyn we spoke of dreams, at Alban Eilir of seeding those dreams. At Calan Mai they were blessed with fertility, creativity. We are now in the midst of their manifestation and paint covers our clothes, our faces are dusty with flour, our fingernails thick with sticky clay. A woman of the Grove asks what is happening, challenging those gathered, and three men step forward and speak of their power.

In eighteenth-century Druidry, the sun was deemed the 'regent of power', the greatest force around which all life revolved. To some extent, of course, this is true. The pathways of our solar system are those of our individual lives as well. The total focus on the sun draws the tradition into a solar-oriented form with the summer solstice its key festival. The darkness, however, has equal potency, leaving the land barren for more than half the year in our temperate climes, holding the tiny stars of the universe in the unmeasurable void of deep and empty space.

The male, solar, Midsummer bias in Druidry is not something that has inspired me or the Grove I celebrate in. Yet the humour remains. One man walks from the east, holding a symbol of his power from that place, such as a sword, a wand, incense, a bird's wing or flight feather, and he speaks of the *awen* of the intellect, of clear sight and knowledge. Another walks forward from the south, with a symbol such as a flame, a sacred dagger, arrow, tooth or claw, and he speaks of the *awen* of courage, strength and vitality. The third steps from the west with a staff, bone or cup, speaking of the *awen* he brings of that place, the wisdom of counsel, experience and direction. If the men walk from south east, south and south west, as they come to the centre they will create the three lines or rays of the *awen* sign.

The woman steps from the north before the men and smiles ...

But the Hag makes her CHALLENGE: Who are you?
The Sun King replies, reflecting back the question.

As the Hag might be seen as the embodiment of winter, so the king of Midsummer is the personification of his season, wild in his tensile strength and smooth self-assurance, casting aside responsibilities, overwhelming and uncompromising. He has the confidence of a man who knows his own power. The woman challenges him to know who he is, so that he can use his power well. The three men might answer, expressing themselves as the light of breath, of laughter, of victory, of passion, of love ... The man in the middle then steps further forward, returning the question. For what is the light but how it is used, reflected off the surface of the pools of our souls, shining in our eyes, absorbed into our cells as life's vitality?

In an intimate rite, all those gathered might then speak of what the sun's inspiration has taught them and how they have expressed that *awen* through their creativity of living.

The *Awen* is called, inspiration sought to answer what the King has asked us. He offers each person the Mask of Flowers so that all may reply.

The mask of flowers is a mask made of flowers, the beauty of our creativity, of our physical growth. We might equate the Calan Mai rite with the blossom buds just opening, while here at Alban Hefin the flowers are at their most exuberant. Holding the mask before our face, we express through our manifested creativity what we have achieved with the sun's *awen*, where our power is being used, our pride and vitality.

As the sun rises just a little to the east once more and the year turns again on its axis, the nights now getting longer, the first petals start to fall. Beneath the petals is the fruit that will swell and ripen for the harvest to come.

The King then offers his Oak Crown to each in the Circle so that they may tie their prayers in golden ribbons to its woven twigs.

The oak, the tree of strength and endurance, the king of our forests, is the symbol of this sun god, and, holding his power now with responsibility, he offers it to each person so that they might use its energy and its wisdom. Infusing the ribbons with intention, tying our emotions into the knots, we adorn the crown with beautiful light, which is reflected back at the sun king. With its ribbons, the crown can then be burned in the ritual fire, the prayers taken into essence, accepted by the spirits, moved through to manifestation. It is an act which is often resisted, but it has a poignancy that can't be ignored. Otherwise the crown is held by the Grove until Gwyl Awst or Alban Elfed, when it is burned with the harvest offerings. Again, in an intimate rite each person might speak aloud their prayers, while in a more open rite, these may be said only with the silent voices of our souls.

How has the sun's inspiration touched our land and our community? The ritual then allows us to acknowledge this.

The Hag and the Sun King bless the Bread and Mead, and in giving the first to each other, they honour the play between light and dark, the battles fought and ceded. She gives to the earth and he to the sun. With blessings they share the feast amongst all those gathered. The Vow of Kinship is spoken, affirming the bond of the community.

With the last prayers, the ritual is closed in the normal way, honouring and giving thanks to the ancestors, the gods and the spirits of place with the four directions. Peace is affirmed and the circle is opened. So the rite ends...

We are in tune with the flow of Alban Hefin's energy when we are both in control and out of control, when our energy is expansive, explosive and extraordinary, and, in letting go into its force, we find our place and our purpose.

Lughnasadh

Pronounced *loo-nuh-suh* in Gaelic, sometimes spelled Lughnasa, this festival is the feast of the sun god Lugh, he of the Skilful Hand, the Irish counterpart to the old British god Llew Llau Gyffes who was equated by the Romans with their Mercury. In Saxon, the festival was called Hlaef-mass, meaning 'loaf mass', now Lammas, the celebration of the first sheaves of the harvest. In Welsh, it is Gwyl Awst, pronounced *gwil-oust*, and translated as 'the feast of August', its traditional calendrical date being the first of the month. For those who place the festivals by the cycle of nature, Gwyl Awst is celebrated with the first loaf made of the freshly harvested wheat.

Of course, for our ancestors, immediately the harvest begins the hard work begins too. It is a time of community, of everyone giving everything they have in terms of time and energy to gather in the crops and get them to market as quickly as possible.

THE RITUAL

This festival rite is often a long and lazy affair, filled with laughter and feasting, baked in the summer sun. The spirits of place are honoured, peace affirmed and the circle is woven gently, loosely (unless otherwise needed), with children running in and out of its boundaries. Scattering wheat and yellow petals for the circle's casting has a potent feel, though once when I did this the result was unrelenting harassment by three hens and their fluffy chicks from a nearby farmyard ...

The incense for consecration might be bright with bergamot and orange blossom, water from a spring or clear local river. The four directions, the spirits of place and ancestors are all honoured in the usual way before the ritual intention is declared and presence affirmed. The declaration of the festival rite is made, clarifying the intention of the gathering.

CHALLENGE: What is this time?
The power and warmth of the Sun has filled the land, as he gave his strength to

care for the people, pouring his golden light into the wheat and barley fields. We come to honour that gift. The Corn King strides around the Circle.

Proud and strong, yet having taken responsibility for his strength at Alban Hefin, the sun god has shone across the land. His progeny, the divine spirit honoured in this rite, holds the beauty of his sacred light reflected, rich with sunshine and with nourishment. This is the corn king and he walks the circle with all the majesty of royalty.

Here might be sung the old folk song John Barleycorn or a Bard of the Grove might play the flute or the drums. There are moments of solemnity and moments of dance perhaps, the women (or men) enticing John to twirl and spin with them to the rhythm of the music and their own personal celebration. I have seen this done in a serenely ceremonial way, formal and dignified, and I have seen the ritual erupt into a wild procession with John at the head of it, proud and silent, with the dancers and children following him laughing wild and free.

A joker is often seen at the rites of Gwyl Awst (he might be present at Calan Gaeaf and other festivals too). His role is not to make those gathered laugh so much as to throw their consciousness into waking through surprise, stupidity, shock or irreverence. He might leap into the circle, collapse, sing or mimic others. A good joker will never take the limelight for more than an instant, slapping us awake then hurling our focus right back onto the key players. He is an observer of the drama, not a character within it. It's a powerful role to play.

Both thanks and honour are offered by all but the joker to the proud and beautiful king, acknowledging his wealth and vigour, all that is now drying to gold in the sun. Any who have brought bread and mead for the rite bow to the king with reverence and lay their gifts at the altar.

The Corn King is slain!

Who actually kills John Barleycorn is not always defined. It may be one of the Grove who plays the Lord of the Land, it may be a priest assigned to the role, or the Hag. With a scythe carefully used or one made of card by the children for the occasion, whoever it is trails the king, bringing him down with a single movement as if cutting the corn. John lies as if dead upon the ground and 'blood' is strewn across his body. This might be water dyed red with beetroot or blood red petals; it is both an image of John's own blood, but more importantly it is the blood sacrifice offered to the spirits of the land and to the gods in thanks for the harvest that is to come. At an intimate rite, menstrual blood might be used, though perhaps not so much thrown on John as offered back to the land as sacrifice.

Thanks are offered once more to the Gods, as Sacrifice is given. The Harvest Wheel is made.

Everyone gathered now lays their sheaf of wheat or barley in the centre of the circle, forming a solar disc or wheel. As they put their sheaf down, they might state what it is they have gained in this harvest. Using just one word, such as 'love', 'acknowledgement', 'certainty' or the like, inspires us to think more clearly, summing up the lessons gained.

When this rite was last done by the Grove before the time of writing, in 1999, the total solar eclipse was less than a fortnight ahead. Three women of the Grove crept silently into the centre of the circle and, as if in slow motion, covered the harvest wheel with a black veil. Only after the Grove had pleaded did they agree to release the harvest light ...

First Fruits are shared.

What people bring to a gathering may be symbolic or a real portion of their 'first fruits' or first sheaves of their harvest. Fresh raspberries, coins, a spoonful of preserves, a handful of peas, a snitch of mint or lavender might be given to each person. The symbol may be placed, scattered or dropped upon the harvest wheel – rose petals of love, milk of new life. A song or story may be shared. The importance of it is that each person is given the opportunity to declare what they have achieved, what they have gained, and so have that recognized by the community, enabling them to own it better and use it well.

A Vow of Kinship is made, the *Awen* called, inspiration sought that we might use

our harvest well. The Bread and Mead are blessed, the alchemical art of transformation honoured. The feast is shared, the first part being given back to the land. Prayers are said, offering healing wherever abundance is not found through natural crisis and war.

At this rite a collection is often made – of food, money or promises – for charities or other causes, so that the abundance shared in the rite is affirmed and flows further, spreading out from the community into many worlds.

If the weather is warm and dry, the celebratory feast and *eisteddfod* will drift on for many hours with stories and poetry, dance and song. When folk need to leave, the ritual is closed with final blessings and prayers, the ancestors are honoured and thanked, together with the gods, the spirits of place and those of the four directions. Peace is affirmed and the circle is opened. So the rite ends ...

The art of transformation that makes wheat into bread takes the grain through the four elemental powers. The bees' work in creating the honey that the brewer transforms into mead is another magical process of transformation. This is an important awareness at this festival and can be used much more extensively than it was in this ritual. Working with the process we can find a symbiotic or empathetic path that will guide us through our own transformation.

Games are often played at Gwyl Awst in the tradition of our ancestors. Races and feats of strength take place. Handfastings, Druid weddings, are also traditional at this time. The folk custom of flaming wheels signifying the turning of the year can still be seen around the country at this festival, as at Midsummer. Rolling cheeses or barrels or any such round thing is also often a part of the Gwyl Awst revelry.

Autumn Equinox

The turning-point in this Lughnasadh season of the harvest, the autumn equinox is again a time when the day and night are of equal length. Occurring at some point between 20 and 23 September, it is known commonly by the Welsh/ Brythonic Alban Elfed, pronounced *elved*, meaning 'light of autumn'. Celebrating the end of the grain harvest, it is the festival of Harvest Home.

I have given seven rituals from the eight in the wheel, seven from those I've celebrated with my Grove over the last year, offering ideas that can be taken and rearranged. I've left huge gaps, giving few words that might be spoken, few images and no locations, most of which when filled in would be in such radically different ways by different people in different places, with different visions and desires, as to make them entirely different rites.

Alban Elfed I will keep open for the reader to create. This festival is one where we acknowledge what it is we have learned and we determine how now we will use it; it seems only appropriate to put that art into practice for this rite as this chapter comes to a close. The basic structure has been given, some or all of which can be used. As to the content of the rite, what would the important features be?

Three challenges might be posed:

❧ What is this time?
❧ What have you harvested?
❧ How will you use it?

The first question tells of the place of balance, encouraging us to observe clearly the worlds around us, searching both for paradox and duality yet also for ways in which those are held tenable, equal, balanced, even if only for moments at a time. In calling the spirits of place and to our ancestors for inspiration, we might find ways in which those paradoxes and balances are reflected in ourselves, accepting the teaching.

The second question asks what it is we have achieved in this cycle of growth that is now coming to an end. Again, looking to the actual harvest of our land is a good beginning. What is all gathered in? What is still being harvested? What of these are staples in our diet? What of these are grown in our neighbourhood? Ensuring that, at least for this festival time, we eat food that is locally grown guides our consciousness better to connect with the flow of *awen* as it shimmers through our environment.

Looking to what it is that we ourselves have harvested is often much harder. The focus of the Earth's harvest will guide us, however, both as a thought and as an altar.

Looking at the apples and pears, bread and beans, grains and seeds laid out in patterns that inspire beauty, expressing the weave of life with their colour and shining energy, we can explore our own sense of value and achievement, held in the arms of the spirits of nature.

The third challenge is one which teaches us of faith, abundance and acceptance. Only when we can truly own our harvest can we work with it responsibly. Only then can we be clear as to what is needed for next year's crop, what must be held back as seed grain. Only then can we feel the freedom of being able to share, to release our grip, free of the fear that it will slip from our fingers, leaving us in the famine of scarcity and degradation, worthless and alone. Only in sharing can we truly receive the gratitude that is positive feedback, building confidence and self-esteem. Only when we know what we have can we celebrate freely without losing responsibility, feasting on our excess in a rich dance of wonder. This challenge guides us to find the inspiration that will teach us the true value of life, beginning with our own.

The challenges addressed, the ritual can be a dance of thanksgiving and celebration. Whom do we need to thank? The spirits of place, of land, sea and sky, the powers of nature, the gods ... and each other.

The ritual feast of this ceremony can be of home-baked bread, as at Gwyl Awst. The mead might here be substituted with local or home-brewed cider or scrumpy, honouring the apples that bring us the sharp sweetness of our lands, concentrated into one delicious bite.

SUNRISE AND SUNSET

It is quite appropriate to perform any of the above rituals just whenever it *seems* appropriate and I have not mentioned in any of them the actual honouring of sunrise or sunset. The exact timing of ritual for this purpose is not something many priests are well known for ... but proceedings are paused while the sun sinks through the final moments of day or breaks across the horizon into another and prayers are said. It happens with perfect synchronicity, every time.

Anyone wishing to add a welcoming of the sun or moon or a farewell at their setting at the end of their path across the sky will find it easy enough to do.

Reverence and respect, a moment's silence, a pause to listen and truly see, spirit to spirit, are all that is needed. Of course, anything more formal, dramatic or poetic can be created. In the main, though, the spectacle is too awe-inspiring to be enhanced by much human ceremonial beyond prayers and song.

Honouring the solar and lunar tide is something that is and can be done every day.

A NOTE ON STYLE

The rites I have given here are, to some extent, held within one style: my own. It is, as is all my Druidic practice, based on spirit to spirit relationship and intuitive understanding, with a focus on healing, personal realization, congruence, responsibility and a love for the environment within which we live.

Each person reading this book will have their own style, though, based on their unique strengths, talents, cravings, priorities and understandings. With many who are musically talented in a group, where the creativity flows in artwork and crafts, where there are children who can be involved in making masks, robes, props and lanterns, where the creation of exquisite food or elegant poetry is an available option, where there are those who can speak the old tongues of Anglo-Saxon, Welsh and Gaelic, the rites may appear quite different. An understanding of astrology, the cusp points of the solar festivals and the fixed elemental powers of the seasonal rites, can also be used, as can the position and phase of the moon and other stars.

Not being physically so strong, I don't automatically push my ritual practice in that direction, yet rites can be very active, weaving in environmental work, hiking into the wild, clearing streams, planting trees. Caring for a piece of land throughout the year offers a perfect focus.

I have not given much on the way in which the old myths of our culture can be woven into festival rituals. There are other books giving the tales and the further reading suggested at the back of the book will guide those who wish to know more. While some Druids might consider work with the gods and heroes essential to celebrating the festivals, my feeling is that working with the spirits of our environment and those of our own ancestors is a more important place to start. Any specific (as opposed to generic) deity or spirit is best invoked only where a personal relationship exists, where there is an openness towards real empathy and an eagerness to listen, to understand, spirit to spirit.

It is the contribution of each individual, soul deep and inspired, that creates a ritual's colour, texture, taste and feel. Only when that is done freely is the ritual true.

rituals for life's
JOURNEY

THE power of death we address in Druidry through our acknowledgement of its presence in nature as we celebrate the passing tide of the year, allowing our minds and bodies to flow with the currents that lead us through harvest's sacrifice and autumnal decay into the season of winter's dying and birthing. At rites such as Samhain/Calan Gaeaf and Alban Arthan we explore consciously fears held around the issues, processing and learning, drawing strength, finding freedom.

As spring comes we find ourselves facing the matter of sexuality, working through the constraints and fears in just the same way, addressing it gently at Alban Eilir and 'full frontal' at Beltane/Calan Mai, symbolically or directly according to what is personally needed or appropriate.

As we will see in the next chapter, though this process in the solar year takes some 365 days, we also have the lunar tide that just takes around 29 days from first offering us the glimpse of a sharp new crescent to its bright ripe fullness to the moments when we are taken back into its dying darkness.

Yet all through the year we are dealing with that other key drive in the human psyche, the fear of change, which provokes our clamp-grip on familiarity or the inverse reaction of constant dismissal and non-commitment. Every ritual guides us through the ongoing shifts and transitions of daily living; in this chapter we look at how the inevitable process of change is better managed in the cycle of our lives as a whole.

Rites of passage are ceremonies that stretch back into the mists of human history. As society grew with tribal culture and evolving human consciousness, we can imagine these rituals to have been simple means by which statements were made, statements of growth and strength, fertility and association. They would have enabled a people to understand and accept more readily the emotionally provocative happenings in life, events brought on by lust and love, hormonal shifts, the leaving or dying of one of their number.

In the same way now, rites of passage are ways of honouring the changes that occur, both those we choose and those that hurl themselves upon us. They encourage us to recognize the ways in which change affects us – both as individuals and as the societies within which we live. While a few rites are performed privately in a solitary fashion, most are celebrated openly, for the witnessing of the rite by the community, family and friends is usually a critical part of its value. Walking through the doorway into a new reality we declare ourselves to have changed, and in so doing we ask those around us to adjust their attitude towards us, so supporting the change and our new life ahead.

In Christian culture just three or four rites are offered throughout a lifetime, depending on the branch of the tradition – the rites of baptism or christening, confirmation or first communion, and those for marriage and death. Islamic and Judaic cultures are similar. In secular culture, there are only the rites of marriage and death, both ceremonies that take less than 20 minutes at a stretch. While these may deal socially with the crises of death and sex, for many they simply don't go far enough. Any other great changes in life are marked with all our society has left: the drinking party.

Hinduism, the Pagan spirituality rooted in the Indian subcontinent, has around eight rites, beginning with those of conception and tracking life's path through to death. In modern European Paganism and Druidry, where there is a less distinct social-traditional framework but still an attitude that demands we honour life with its flow of energy, the number of rites varies to whatever is needed.

Any period or moment of change can be affirmed and celebrated through a rite of passage. A welcoming or farewell, a coming together or a parting, an event that brings great joy and one that evokes fear or grief, there are no occasions in our living not appropriate to acknowledge through a spiritual ritual. When transitions have not been adequately recognized, leaving a sense of loss and lack of conclusion, rites can be done in retrospect, allowing us to find the present and move on with confidence.

Beginning with that understanding, let us look at the basic form.

THE THREE STEPS

A rite of passage can be a momentary pause in daily life as we acknowledge a shift as it is taking place around and within us, as we find ourselves needing to register and affirm it. Vows might then be made between ourselves and other souls, spirits or deities. Any such rite is always witnessed by the spirits of place and the ancestors, particularly those invoked, even if we choose to make the statement alone. Often these solitary rites are avowed more powerfully at a later stage within a ritual that is witnessed by our community, friends and family. Though sometimes this is not necessary or even appropriate, doing so usually exquisitely reinforces our own private actions. Making a ritual 'public' can take a tremendous amount of courage, yet these are often the most powerful and deeply transformative rites.

If performed as a full ritual, witnessed and shared, the rite of passage can be held within the structure laid out in Chapter Seven and used as the framework for the festival rites of the previous chapter. Whether we make our declaration of change in this longer form or as a momentary ritual, the central part of the rite, its focus and process, will be the same. This can be put simply as the following:

THE CHALLENGE: WHY ARE YOU HERE?

We begin any rite of passage with looking back, understanding where we have come from and all that we have gained in wealth and learning from our experiences. Acknowledging the past, we work to accept its reality, first dealing with the positive aspects, and finding our strength and centre in doing so – even if these will be shifted as we pass through the rite to a new world ahead.

It is important that we honour those spirits who have guided us through the past, beginning with our ancestors, then those living around us, all who have supported and taught us, giving us what we have needed and helping to create what we are today. We honour too the spirits of the environment within which we have

lived, through which we have passed, for their influence too has formed our life, bringing us to this moment of change. In honouring the past, perceiving clearly the sacred, we might make offerings to express and affirm our gratitude.

Once we have explored the positive, we move to the negative. By this I don't mean the hard times that have been our teachers. The negative is what is now redundant. As we have grown and our life has changed, there will be aspects that we no longer want to carry with us. The rite may be primarily about letting these elements go, about casting off the old burdens and being reborn or reawakening in a new reality. There will also be other negative issues, the side-effects of a life we no longer wish to lead. At this time – once acknowledged – the dross can be released.

Essentially, it is the redundant that brings us to needing the moment of the ritual; the 'Why?' is usually answered with the declaration of what will be put behind us.

THE CHALLENGE: ARE YOU READY TO CHANGE?

Once the negative issues have been recognized, together with the reason why the rite has been declared (the ritual's intention), we bring ourselves into the present. The challenge is made by asking what will be needed in a new reality: the stability and trust, the wisdom, the independence, the strength or courage, the releasing and caring, whatever it may be.

The challenge might be made gently and indirectly, or as a clear confrontation, a 'What gives you the right to ask us to accept your changing?!' Are you really ready to let go of what has been familiar? When the pain of change kicks in, the ache of releasing and facing those unknown trackways, will you hold to your course?

Then the gateway is revealed. In the drama of ritual this is often given some tangible form – an archway made of arms, a hoop made of woven branches, a sword over which to step, or some other appropriate form. It may be a series of tasks to perform, a feat that needs to be accomplished. It may be easy to get through; it may be frightening, alarmingly hard, entangled with problems that must be solved. Some may be created by the tribe or priest who challenges, some by the spirits of place or the ancestors openly expressing the blocks to be surmounted; the witnesses to a rite may be helpful or provocative. Obstacles to the gateway are an intrinsic part of that very changing process we are so determinedly clambering through.

In some rituals, it is important to offer vows as assertions of our resolve to make it to the other side. We are assuring the spirits that we will honour ourselves and those around us, and in doing so asking for their guidance and support through the actual process of change.

THE CELEBRATION: THE MOVING ON

Once through the gateway, the first thing we do is recognize what we have done. Here, too, vows might be made. Standing on the edge of our future, having declared that this new day will be clearly different from yesterday, we affirm this to be true with vows made to our gods.

If those who are witnessing the rite are pleased that we have truly moved from one place to another, the change is openly acknowledged. Gifts may be given, blessings, tokens of love and support. Tools may be offered for the journey to come by those who have already been exploring its landscape.

The change is then celebrated in whatever way is appropriate to the event and the gathering. Music and dance, feasting and storytelling may take place, either within the *nemeton* cast for the rite or outside the consecrated space. However formally or spontaneously this is done, the value is important: the celebration allows an emotional release of energy that acts as a final seal of approval.

With a vision of how a rite is created, let us look at specific rites of passage and see how the process fits together.

First Rites

The first rites of passage are those for the arrival of a new life.

Understanding that, through the cycles and flow of existence, our ancestors are also our descendants, a couple hoping for a child might make prayers and offerings to their ancestors and their gods, or some more formal ritual, in order to invite a spirit to join them. The rites are often tender and emotional, particularly if the couple have been trying to conceive for some time. Because in Paganism there is an acknowledgement that it is the creative energy of a spirit that is the spark of conception, the physical act of making love is seen only as the crafting of a doorway, an opportunity thrown open for a spirit to walk through. If the occasion is rich with love and beauty, shining with well-being, the doorway reflects this; love is therefore a way for the couple to honour the spirit, the ancestors, the process. Of course, sometimes we open that door just a crack and some spirit who has been lingering, waiting, slips in. Sometimes, however beautiful and welcoming the couple can make it, the opportunity is not taken up.

When conception does happen, rituals are often done. These are a weaving of the acknowledgement and acceptance of change with the thanksgiving and welcoming of the spirit who has inspired conception. It is a gentle time, full of anticipation, and the rites are usually fairly private affairs, strengthening the bond, affirming that all is well and the change will be accepted, nurtured, supported. A candle or stone is often used as an anchor, a particular essential oil (tangerine is a favourite) or piece of music, something that through the ritual becomes a source of calm and strength, stability and certainty, so that every time it is held, burned or played, the magical positive energy of the rite is accessed again.

While it is most usual for a spirit to commit and connect more fully with the physical body it will live with at between 8 and 14 weeks after conception, sometimes the spirit holds back, indecisive. Some spirits don't entirely commit until after the birth, creating complications that are physical and/or emotional. When a spirit pulls out, withdrawing its life force, the foetus miscarries or is stillborn. More often than not, it is the spirit's decision to leave and in Druidry this is understood with the acceptance that birth is a great deal harder than death. Less often, miscarriages are caused by accident or genetic/physical problems, though when this happens the grief is quite different, the spirit also expressing the deep sadness of loss. The rites used in these cases are those of dying.

With modern birthing practice still too centred around the intrusive and male-oriented medical profession, an increasing number of women are actively choosing natural birth, being conscious of the environment within which they welcome a new child. Keeping a newborn warm, the lights dim, the noise levels soft and allowing the child the skin to skin contact, the heart rhythms and soul nourishment of the breast as soon as is possible, will honour the spirit that has just made the most challenging and painful journey.

Presenting offerings of thanks to the guiding spirits and to the gods is a simple act that makes a tremendous difference. During those first weeks when the mother's focus has slipped from her partner to her new child, the father's role is one of holding the intimate and sacred space secure: as the mother holds the child, so the father holds the mother. Performing a ritual that affirms this is an empowering way for him to contribute when otherwise he might feel frustrated or displaced, not able adequately to help. Where there is no father or caring partner, making offerings secures the *nemeton* necessary for those first days, weeks or months of new life.

THE WELCOMING AND NAMING RITE

In most cases, the first official rite of a lifetime is the child's Welcoming and Naming Rite. In Druidry this is not an opportunity to dedicate the child to a particular god or promise to bring it up within a certain religious tradition, both of which are antipathetic to the basic tenets of the spirituality, the honouring of an individual's own flow of *awen*. A Welcoming Rite is in many ways simply a thanksgiving, a time to have a new life blessed by the spirits of place, the powers of nature. It is an important way in which a child is accepted by the community. The tremendous change another life can make on any group of people is seldom honestly and openly acknowledged, and a rite guides all through the process of change. Particularly when the child is their first, the rite gives a couple a chance to acknowledge the upheaval in their lives and to have that change acknowledged, honoured and supported by their families, friends and community.

Here is the first of a number of images, incomplete in its detail but expressing colour and texture that might inspire ...

As the musicians played the last of the song, the vocalist, her eyes closed, her face washed with sunshine, hummed as if singing with the trees and I walked to the altar, my voice joining hers as I sang to the spirits of place, rich harmony. Old oaks rimmed the meadow, boughs of elder beneath them, heavy with dark berries, and as I called, asking them to hold the circle in the sanctity of their *nemeton*, I felt the warmth of their laughter in the breeze. It poured through me, glowing.

The children, dressed in Sunday best, came forward as I beckoned, holding their baskets in uncertain fingers, and I crouched as I called again to the spirits of the land, to the foxes, the badgers, the swallows of the open skies, the blackbirds, bees and tiny beetles, and the little girl's eyes opened wide. The children scattered the offerings, nuts and seeds, and parents in the circle around us smiled.

Declaring the rite, the mother stepped forward, shy but proud, and I watched as she spoke, brimming with awe at the essence of her role. As her own mother joined her, touching her hair with affection, a few more of the circle sat down on the grass, looking up, watching, as the women spoke of motherhood, giving thanks. Sharing.

The baby was reaching out for her mother, softly whimpering when she returned to the circle's edge, and I spoke of the ancestors, honouring the blood-line into which the child was born. Family members stood forward and stories were told of grandparents, great grandparents, and when the mother's brother spoke of her she blushed and laughter washed through. The band played another song, languid in the sunshine, and she fed the baby, listening, wrapped in the veils of her focus and joy.

When she stood again to make her commitment, vowing to care for her son, to give him all that she could while honouring herself, it was hard not to wonder how many in the gathering were thinking of the child's father. He'd turned his back, walked away. I watched the colour shifting, a sadness painted bright with determination, and prayed for guidance. Yet as those asked to make a special commitment stepped forward to declare their vows, offering their support, their friendship, wit and wisdom, giving their gifts, the bitter energy melted, dissolving in the sunshine, leaving smiles that expressed each soul's honesty and wonder.

The mother herself was the one who touched the child to the earth. Holding him gently, she knelt so that he lay on the sunlit grass as, crouching, I called to the powers of earth, the goddess of the dark soil, of the womb of creation, asking for blessings upon his body, his soul, his life. A young cousin held out the raspberries and, squeezing a few between my fingertips, I touched his forehead with the red juice, making the sign of the *awen*, whispering, 'Sweetness of the fruits of living.'

The child's father had disappeared, abdicating his responsibility, yet his parents had not. The paternal grandfather, his lips pursed as he waited for my sign, nodded as I smiled at him and walked forward to take the child gently in his arms. Lifting him up into the air, he beamed with pride, the breeze catching a soft tuft of the baby's hair, and I called to the powers of sun and sky, the god of light and freedom's knowing, asking for blessings.

When we called for the powers of the seas to bless the child, it was the baby's aunt who held him, touching his little body with drops of water held in a bowl of seashells by her son, another cousin, as she spoke the words of the old Scottish prayer:

A small wave for your form
A small wave for your voice
A small wave for your speech
A small wave for your means
A small wave for your generosity
A small wave for your appetite
A small wave for your wealth
A small wave for your life
A small wave for your health
Nine waves of grace upon you.
Waves of the Giver of Health.
(CG)

As the band played again, I looked around those gathered and saw the local vicar, his head to one side, smiling, his fingers tapping on his knee. I closed my eyes and felt the sunshine's warmth in the rhythm of the music.

Such a rite would continue with the giving of the child's name. While we realize that the child might grow and find his own name, the Naming Rite is when the parents or carers offer a name as a special gift. The power of a name is acknowledged, for it holds its own energy, its history and meaning, giving us a place in our community. The rite is an opportunity for the parents to present the child to all

Ritual

those who have gathered, and as a named individual he is then accepted and officially welcomed.

The rite would close as any other, with first the celebratory feast of bread and mead (or an alternative), then the thanksgivings and the honouring of the spirits. While some babies' rites are filled with children, others are for the first of a community when there are few in the circle. A rite can obviously be geared more towards the children if it is felt important to keep them interested and attentive.

In the mid 1990s, part of a blessing was given to the Gorsedd of Caer Abiri from a hereditary line of Druids. It has subsequently been used to bless hundreds of children in the community, the four elemental powers invoked with the appropriate verses:

I baptize thee with Mother Earth
From whose loins we come
And to whose arms we fly
When our journey here is over

I baptize thee with the winds
That come from the four corners
Of the Earth, the winds that
Scatter the seeds of the Harvest
And blow away the snows of Winter

I baptize thee with fire
So that thy spirit may be
Purified, and thy days
Be long and fruitful

I baptize thee with the waters
Of life, the waters that no
Living thing can do without

 Rituals for Life's Journey

Give thanks to our Lady
For thy bounteous Harvest
And may She bless and keep you
All the days of your life.
(SB)

Rites of Childhood

The first years of childhood are filled with changes, both for the child and its parents, and ritual moments are ways that re-establish clarity in the midst of mayhem. Longer rituals of the early period tend to focus on the parents and their ability to move with these changes, to adapt and learn. Rites remind us to hold the *nemeton* through everyday life, ensuring the child might always know the freedom of safe space and the clarity of boundaries, allowing the soul to grow in its own uniqueness. Rites guide a child to know the power of perceiving the world as sacred, to know respect for life. We teach children to walk softly. The rituals of childhood help us to gradually relinquish the reins of responsibility for that child's *nemeton*, with its scary edges.

Whenever a child is aware of doing something for the first time, a pause to explore and acknowledge the moment is beautifully potent. In doing so we honour the past dependency, the present growth and the future's potential, encouraging the child with every step he takes. In honouring the sacred, acknowledging change and growth, making offerings of thanks, we are respecting the child, the ancestors and ourselves.

If the child is to go to school, the first days often bring difficulties for everyone. The parents' releasing and the child's adventuring alone can both be alleviated by the simple process of a ritual. An exquisite gift is usually made to the child during this rite, an item that he can take or wear that will act as a source of inspiration, reminding him of the stability and strength he has within himself, reminding him of the ritual when his family acknowledged him as brave enough to make the journey, reminding him that he is supported, loved. Home-crafted badges, bracelets or belts are suitable, as is anything that won't be easily mislaid and is acceptable within 'school rules'. The process of making the item can be an important part of the rite.

Ritual

Losing the first tooth is also a significant time. Now the child, usually aged between five and seven, is starting to see the world through more independent eyes.

Holding his lantern he walked with six-year-old solemnity, lifting his hand to the trees, the candle flickering as he read, 'Spirits of the north, I ask for your blessings, the strength of the bull, the night senses of the bat, at this time of rebirth.' He lowered his hand and bowed silently, his blond head touched by the firelight. Stumbling a little in the darkness, he frowned and made his way to the birch tree. 'Spirits of the east, I ask for your blessings, the agility of the lapwing, the freedom of the buzzard, at this time of awakening.' Eyes closed, I listened to his voice, calling in the south, for the 'stealth of the fox, the courage of the wild cat', words he had chosen in the days of preparing for this moment, 'this time of change'. In the west he smiled at me, knowing this was my favourite, as he asked the spirits for 'the gentleness of the whale, the laughter of the otter, at this time of thanks … thanksgiving'.

On the log by the fire he sat talking about everything he felt he'd learnt in his six years. We watched the flames and heard his words. His focus was shifting, growing away from me, from the protection I could offer. He looked up at his father, his green eyes shining. They were so alike. When he gave his offerings, he did so knowing that he was the centre of attention yet without games of pretension. Wanting to do it properly, he turned to me for guidance and, when I smiled, he beamed at his dad with pride.

Asking him if he were ready to start the second cycle of his life I was all too aware of asking myself, too, if I were ready to let go just a little more. He frowned, and nodded carefully. I looked at his father across the fire, my partner, lover. I hadn't realized how hard this would be and, as my son walked towards him, I breathed in deeply.

His words were beautiful.

'It is with great honour that I take your hand and walk with you the next part of your life. May the gods guide me that we may know what is of true value, that we may know how to speak our truth to each other with honour and respect, how to walk our talk, how to give and how to receive. May I guide you well that you may ever be proud that I am your father.'

Tears filled my eyes.

As children learn to take more and more responsibility for themselves, the rites of passage begin to mean more to them as individuals. There is a stage in many children's lives, however, when being the focus of such a rite is far from what they want. A rite of passage to a pre-teen is often more about the quadbike track or pyjama party. This doesn't mean that the rites aren't of value for the parents though ... Using ritual we facilitate, by acknowledgment, acceptance and affirmation, the tangled process that is the weave of internal and external change.

First Rites of Adulthood

Rituals that act as marker points for the changing times of puberty are some of the most difficult yet most necessary. Part of the problem in modern culture is the confusion about adulthood. To our ancestors, the puberty shift that brings menstruation in girls and, in boys, the testicles dropping, the voice breaking, the first real wet dreams, may have been a clear sign of the transition between childhood adventures and adult responsibilities, and as such a 'ritual' acceptance of the change was inbuilt with the changing expectations and roles played by the individuals. This is no longer the case; what follows the hormonal upheaval is the trauma we now call adolescence.

Not only are kids coping with the physical changes, but the emotional tides can be utterly overwhelming, particularly so when creative and accepted outlets for adult energy, aggression and sexuality are difficult to find. To know that there is support at this time, and support coming from a place of intimate and sacred space, can make the difference between a rebellious nightmare and positive conscious growth.

FIRST BLOODS RITE

Talking to women about ritual, one of the most common regrets is the lack of clear acknowledgement and guidance given at the time of their first bleeding cycle. In a world that holds the male mentality that equates blood with damage, woundedness, weakness, the tides of fertility in women are still secreted away as taboo. While once generations of girls began their bleeding without any guiding knowledge at all, now television advertising for 'sanitary' products designed to 'protect' us from what some still call the 'curse' use clear blue dyed water to imitate blood. We are still encouraged in every way possible to pretend the bleeding simply isn't happening. Girls start to smoke, use make-up and jewellery at uncomfortably early ages, searching for an acknowledgement of their shifting state, yet the one truth they have which proves they are growing up they are forced to hide behind the screens of a screaming silent prohibition.

The Menarche or First Bloods Rite is for some the most powerful of their lives. It overtly declares to the community that a girl has passed into the second stage of her life: her fertile years. The responsibility of her fertility is enormous. With it she has the power to create a new life and the power to shatter lives, including her own. It is a critical time at which to offer to a girl the guidance and support of the women whom she respects, acknowledging this new power that changes her status, sharing wisdom, tears and laughter. The rite celebrates the girl's transition in whatever way is appropriate for the group. It is usually not open to any male or to girls who have not yet begun their tides. The celebration is first about inviting the new initiate into the laughter of a healthy adult world – a place of responsibility where life is honoured.

At this time when childish things are kicked away with a hormonal scowl, childhood is celebrated. We explore with the girl its value and delights, its sharpest and softest lessons. Preparing for the rite is important, particularly with a girl who is responding badly to apparent pressure. Allowing her to delve again into her childhood freedom – from an adult perspective – is precious. Using her creativity, either alone or within the group who are supporting her transition, paint-splashed and tangled in coloured threads, laughter and glue, she might be encouraged to make something for the rite – a robe, offerings, a blood bowl, mask or pouch. Some girls will use flowers and poetry rich with beauty. Others will need to express themselves with wild body paint and images of their mortality. It is important that while the rite is held by the adult supporters, they are wholly accepting of the girl's current experience.

Honouring childhood in the rite, the women then guide the girl to understand the changes that are happening, physically and emotionally, to explore and enjoy the reality of her blood tides. This might be done ritually, poetically, or by each woman offering a gift of advice, a story. The girl is handed the challenge to break the taboo our society has laid upon women's bleeding, to touch the blood, knowing its power is that of her fertility, of her body's health and strength. In the rite she might have a cup of her own menstrual blood and with it she may paint her body with her own secret signs, with *awens* or hearts to be washed off later in the course of the day. She might offer her blood back to the earth, or into the sea or a river that flows to the coast, acknowledging the web that connects us with nature.

Through this challenge to work with her blood creatively, consciously, those with the girl offer her too the challenge of being a woman. What does it entail? What is this responsibility and how can it be freeing, exciting, empowering? The girl is challenged to live life to the full, with freedom and courage, honesty and self-acceptance, always knowing and learning the value of the women's circle, its co-operation, support, compassion, riding the waves, the tides of the moon.

Within a spiritual tradition such as Druidry, the ritual is seen as an initiation, the girl walking through a gateway into a new life and being given gifts by the priestess and other women that will be important tools all her life, sources of inspiration, wisdom and community. Ruby and bloodstone are often given as stones or jewellery. The girl may be presented with special blood pads (as opposed to the environmentally compromising disposables) which can be used to collect blood to give back to the earth with prayers each cycle, or a diary or journal, a pouch for beautiful treasures, a moon calendar ... There is no pressure to conform to anything in the ritual. Its focus is to acknowledge the girl's own growth and offer her the most powerful challenge, that of her fertility. There is no greater gift than the acceptance of this power.

Often the girl will take a few days to allow the rite to settle within herself, as if in privacy and quiet she is processing its wonder. Occasionally, where she has close friends who would understand, her celebration will be shared with them.

An old Gaelic prayer, said for the girl by her mother, can be used in these rites:

I bathe thy palms
In showers of wine
In the lustral fire
In the seven elements

In the juice of the rasps
In the milk of honey

And I place the nine pure choice graces
In thy fair fond face
The grace of form
The grace of voice
The grace of fortune
The grace of goodness
The grace of wisdom
The grace of charity
The grace of choice maidenliness
The grace of whole-souled loveliness
The grace of goodly speech
(CG)

As a woman, needless to say, I have never attended a Manhood Rite. Furthermore, in the tradition it is considered intrusive to ask, invading intimate space, pushing at boundaries of confidentiality. On the whole more has been written of Menarche, but my understanding is that in the men's rites much the same process is involved. Honouring the childhood that is now coming to its close, the boy is challenged as to whether he is ready to enter the world of men. Some tests of courage, endurance, strength and wit are posed, the nature of what is to be accomplished adjusting according to the lad, with his natural skills being well utilized and his potential encouraged. Acceptance and celebration are the keys.

FIRST EXPERIENCE OF SEX

Ritual to acknowledge the first experience of sex is not often performed, but may be done privately, perhaps just between a parent and child, or amongst friends. Sometimes it is felt that enough was done at a puberty rite, with the advice given and responsibility accepted. Sometimes, though, the puberty rite will have been performed too early for sexuality to have been brought up sufficiently.

Whether the rite is a formal affair or momentary pause that is shared, exploring sexuality or losing virginity is another step forward that can be soothed with a serious and respectful acknowledgement offered to the individual by those closest to them. Sometimes no decision is made beyond agreeing to walk together, or go out and eat together, but in some way a sacred sanctuary of intimate space is created, through trust and support, and stories are shared and advice given if requested. As always, gifts and offerings make formal the acceptance, support and empathy.

Where the situation is difficult because of shifting perspectives, the Druid attitude to look always for sources of inspiration, unblocking flows of creativity, allows us to find ways of sharing the learning. Each of us accesses the *awen* at different wells of life energy.

Rites of Union

Relationship is a central issue of Druidry. Connected through a network of energy, we influence, if unconsciously, the world around us with all we do (and we are each responsible for what we pour into creation). When consciously we connect with another, spirit to spirit, the level we share increases. Connecting within the circle of our intimate space, that flow of energy is intensified. When we touch, skin to skin, the exchange heightens still further.

Having sex without soul intimacy is possible, if not particularly healthy, the *nemeton* of our sacred space having been withdrawn deep within ourselves, allowing our body to be touched without our soul presence. The boundaries of our intimate circle are our strongest protection and without them secure we lie open to all kinds of abuse. The abuse that occurs *within* the circle of our intimate space is more damaging than anything else.

So it is that we dance on the edge between the protection of our soul's vulnerability and the freedom of love, intimacy and trust. Learning to centre within our spirit strength, being conscious of the boundaries of our intimate space and of our honest intentions, we are able to explore new ground. Learning the art of trust and the power of the *nemeton*, we can reach deeper into relationship, exploring the ecstasy of sharing energy on an intimate level, through love, through give and take, through fantasy, through sexuality.

These critical points of soul growth and freedom are a part of the adventures of Calan Mai, yet in the tradition sexuality is always considered sacred. It might be said that to a Druid every sexual connection is a ritual act – not necessarily formal or ceremonially played out, but always interwoven with honour and respect for the powers of nature that infuse and inspire us, always a quest for beauty, power and vitality, for the sources of *awen*.

Any nature-based spirituality has within it a large element that is pure fertility religion. With every act of love-making, we are mirroring the dance of duality and fertility within the natural world around us, encouraging its rich abundance as it encourages ours. Yet sexuality is only partially about the fertility of creating new life. The art of giving and receiving pleasure, body and soul, is in many ways more accurate a vision of Druid spirituality. Laughter, beauty, dance and nourishment, playfulness and music, poetry and love all contribute to this quest for pleasure. Not surprisingly the art of good relationship which offers sacred and inspiring sexuality is considered an exquisite treasure.

Crafting our love-making as sacred is easily done purely by intention. Honouring the moment, creating a *nemeton* with candles, stones, flower petals or some other gift of beauty, respecting the soul with whom we will share, perceiving that soul's spirit and divine nature, and releasing ourselves into the experience of wonder, we are able to give ourselves, our sensuality and our loving as a gift, an offering, to the gods, the ancestors and all who have inspired the relationship into being.

The exchange of ecstasy within intimate loving space is a powerful gift of *awen*.

MARRIAGE

Committing ourselves to a relationship is a strange and difficult art. Yet to legally bind ourselves into one can cost less than £100, take barely 20 minutes ... and then cost thousands of pounds and many years to extricate ourselves from. The balance is awry.

In Druidry, marriage is understood to be a commitment of support, honour and love, made between two souls and witnessed by the community, by friends and family, and also by the ancestors and the spirits of the land, sea and skies. If we want a legal contract, it can be drawn up by a solicitor or civil servant who registers marriages, but marriage is essentially not about deals, contracts and liabilities, all of which silently underlie the state ceremony.

Sometimes called the Handfasting Rite, a marriage ritual in Druidry is about creating the *nemeton*, a sacred place of intimate exchange, within which the couple can declare the vows of their commitment. This is the heart of the ritual. As vows they write themselves, not idealistic intangibles, these are real promises made about the way that they both perceive the relationship, what they will expect of it and how they will behave within it.

As relationship in Druidry is considered to be spirit to spirit, soul to soul, there is no question with regard to the gender of those marrying. To query the validity of a single sex marriage is anathema to Druidry.

The ritual can be held within the usual structure laid out in Chapter Seven. It is vital to ensure that ancestors, grandparents and relations both present and not present are well honoured, so bringing the families as a whole together in spirit, so that both can accept the union. If the couple want to add a little more 'tradition', the groom and his best man can wait at the circle's edge and only when the sacred space is cast, consecrated and the spirits honoured, does the bride, with her father and attendants, make her entrance ...

The Bard makes a flourish as the pipes drop from his mouth into his other hand and he calls out, a wicked smile upon his face, 'Ah, so now comes the maid, and is she the fairest? Yeh, so would I say! But who this fine day would be the one to give her away?' She looks down, flushing beneath her veil, not from the Bard's words but before the gaze of her groom, now seeing her for the first time in the dress and flowers. Her father clasps her hand a little tighter and she looks up into his face. He nods, breathing in, finding his courage to let go, and he whispers, looking into her eyes, 'I do.' Again the Bard skips and spins, landing before them, bowing. 'Then let the deed be done!'

As they enter the *nemeton* defined by crabapple boughs, flowers and lanterns, the bridesmaids behind them, a stillness settles over the hundred or so people who have gathered in the circle around us. They watch, enchanted, the sound of the brook softening the quiet, the crackling of the fire drawing the focus.

In any rite of transition, where blessings are called for, it is lovely to walk to the four directions and call to the spirits and powers of each element in turn, asking that their wisdom may infuse the subject of the rite. In a wedding rite, the couple often stand before each quarter and, acknowledging the spirits, receive (for example) blessings of freedom, knowledge and rebirth in the east, vitality, courage and warmth in the south, love, flexibility and direction in the west, stability, fertility and nourishment in the north. These might be accompanied by gifts and accepted with offerings of thanks.

The word 'handfasting' comes of the tradition, still sometimes used, of wrapping or binding the couple's hands with a length of cloth or cord as they exchange their vows. In the rite I offer, three vows are asked of the couple as well as the ones they give each other, the first two being:

As the Sun and Moon bring light to the Earth, do you vow to bring the light of love and joy to this your union?

Do you vow to honour each other as you honour that which you hold most sacred?

(BDO)

The last is vowed upon the Wedding Stone after the couple have sworn their own vows and exchanged the rings that will symbolize for them the cycles of nature and the *nemeton* of their union. The stone can be a precious gem, a great chunk of flint, a beach pebble or slab of rock, whatever seems appropriate. It can be kept on the altar or built into their house. The last vow is as follows:

This sacred earth is our home, offering us the power of life, nourishing us, body and soul, holding us from birth until we let go once more into the worlds of spirit. Each rock and stone, each pebble and gem contains within it the stories of all time. You have chosen this as a foundation stone of your marriage. Do you now swear upon it, as a symbol of this sacred land and our holy Mother Earth, to keep your vows?

(BDO)

In any rite of passage or declaration where vows are made, a stone can be used in just the same way. Druidry has no book of scriptures but the landscape within which we live.

Her head back, I see her soul let go into his hands that hold her, this feisty young woman who few would dare cross, and as I glance around the circle I realize many have seen the same. The gift of witnessing such love and trust is offered each one of us as they kiss, held within the *nemeton* of their sacred circle, freed beyond inhibition, sealing their vows.

Entranced by the moment I forget what must happen next, until the big blue eyes of a young bridesmaid bring me back, glaring at me, questioning with impatience. *Yes*, I nod, and her face breaks into a wide shining smile as she tugs at the other's sleeve and the two girls take great handfuls from their baskets, showering rose petals and wheatgrain over the kissing couple.

'Blessings of beauty, of love and fertility ...'

A rite that is rich with joy very often ends after the sharing of bread and mead with a moment when the circle of those gathered is affirmed, perhaps by all holding hands, and prayers are said, offering the special energy of the ritual out into the world so that others may share it, inspired by its beauty.

We change, life hurls us into new experiences and we adapt. We grow and explore wild new lands. When a relationship is strong, when communication flows freely and honestly, it is possible to grow in harmony, moving side by side on the tracks of our adventures. Because, in Druid weddings, we have created our own vows, a relationship might reach a point where the new elements and understandings need to be woven into the commitment. This is often done by holding another marriage ceremony, a rededication that allows us to deepen and update our sacred vows, taking into account our changing worlds. We do this not only to affirm the strength of our relationship, but also to declare to our community the different level on which we are committing, sharing with those around us the joy of our breakthroughs, our deepening love.

RITE OF PARTING

When changes start to undo the knots of a relationship, sometimes the positive way forward is to separate. If a marriage is accompanied by a legal contract, leaving it can be complicated further. It's most usually a desperately traumatic time and, though lawyers can be useful if we are searching for help financially or with child custodies, often they act simply as a part of a culture where marriage is based in social legalities, not relationship.

In Druidry, a couple wishing to end a marriage are offered a Rite of Parting. In its simplest form this is the act of returning to the place where their marriage was vowed, often with the same priest. There the couple must honour each other, in words or actions, maybe a silent bow or significant gift. It can be a time of tears and deep soul pain. Yet if the honouring is not done – at least in intention – the priest will not accept that the relationship is over. If the priest is satisfied that both are ready to let go, thanks are given to all those who witnessed the Handfasting, the spirits of place, the ancestors and (in spirit, for they are not usually present) those who attended in body. The priests asks if the couple are ready to cut the ties. When they are, they turn their backs and walk away.

It's horrendously difficult to do. Yet by affirming that it is done, the grieving is eased.

Rites of Elderhood

Rites of passage can be done for any transition in life. Changing job, passing exams, moving house, finishing a project, concluding an adventure, acknowledging a big lesson learnt, even a significant birthday can all be honoured, acknowledged and celebrated with ritual. Remembering the basic form, the ritual space is created in order for the transition to be made and witnessed within the safety of intimate space.

The key rites of the last era of life are called Rites of Elderhood. In a woman these rites usually acknowledge her transition out of fertility. Often celebrated when a woman has passed through nine moons or cycles without bleeding, such a rite allows her to review her life, its achievements and failures, loves and traumas. She is particularly encouraged to look at what she has created through her years of fertility, both in terms of children and otherwise. When there are no children, this might be a time to honour that too and grieve if there is a sense of loss.

The process of putting the past behind can be made more effective by some symbolic act such as burning diaries or a written overview, a painting or mask, a collage of life. As always, the more emotion that is infused into the making of this object to be released, the more effective the letting go.

In any Rite of Elderhood, the honouring of the ancestors is a key part. We thank them for their teachings and guidance, for the lessons passed on, womb to womb, for finding ourselves in the position of being the older members of the community. In honouring our own experience of life, we can share that experience, guiding others without judgement.

At first she struggled, then realizing what was happening she surrendered, shaking her head, half laughing and half cursing under her breath, as four women wove the balls of wool between and around her legs, round and around. She swayed, losing her balance, and someone grabbed her before she fell as she murmured, 'Bloody hell, how am I going to get out of this one?!'

We stood back, a circle of her friends beneath the trees in the dusk, with me as her priestess. Nobody said a word. She looked down at her legs, bound in a tangle of coloured threads. Her best friend walked forward and their eyes met. It was delicious.

'So d'you really expect us to listen to you now? You think you've something to say, some new status inferred by all your years of living, just because you've burnt the figure you made and the kids have left home and you haven't bled for nearly a year... Huh?'

'Er...' She nearly laughed. Then she realized it wasn't remotely funny.

There was a silence. A waiting.

Her friend stepped over to the ring of hazel, picking it up from the damp grass.

Tied up, the woman again looked down at her legs. Her expression began to change. And bending over with all the dignity of her 49 years she hopped, or rather bounced, across the circle, picking up a knife that lay with the apples beside the altar. As she sheared through the wool, the circle erupted into laughter.

Striding over to her friend, she murmured, 'Nobody's bloody going to tie me down again. Where's that hazel hoop? I'm going through...'

For men, the Rite of Elderhood is less clearly marked, the hormonal changes not being obvious in the changing blood tides. Nor is there the same shift out of fertility. Yet a man's role still changes; slowly he becomes aware of having to give way to the strength and speed of younger men. He moves from being the leader to the observer, the guide. Relationships change and in a ritual shared with others it is often a poignant moment when each person steps forward to speak of their relationship with the subject of the rite. It is a time of gifts, thanksgivings and respect.

Retiring from work is another huge change for many at this time, taking a person into a different social status and one that may at first seem of somewhat less value than what they are used to. It's an important time for the community to honour change.

Last Rites

If someone is aware that death is approaching, many moments arise, times to pause and acknowledge the transition, enabling the process of release, clarifying relationships, giving thanks for all we have gained. The first pathways after death are cast and scripted according to our expectations as to what will happen when we die, taking us gently through our human beliefs and out into the unformed ether beyond time and space. Preparation for dying, in terms of ritual moments or ceremony, is about acknowledging these guiding beliefs, the positive and the negative, the frightening and inspiring. By addressing them in the intimate space of sacred circle, a supportive environment is offered that enables the dying to leave calmly and lovingly.

When someone dies it takes around three days before he is able to detach from the life he has led, gaining an overview and an objectivity. These are important days for the soul who is departing. The traditional time spent with the body laid out is a time to talk, to find strength and hope, forgiveness and gratitude. Prayers and offerings, conversations, lighted candles all make a difference, smoothing the journey. This is our opportunity to help the soul let go.

While various legalities need to be adhered to when somebody dies, it is quite possible for a Druid funeral rite to be held. The non-denominational chapel found in most cemeteries and crematoriums cannot object, nor would they at natural burial grounds. As the time of grieving, however, is often a tender affair, more than one rite is sometimes held in order to honour different religious needs. If the body was cremated, the scattering of the ashes is often a poignant time for a memorial rite to be celebrated.

RITE OF PASSING

The Druid Rite of Passing works within the basic framework, the call to the ancestors of blood being especially poignant at this time. In the rite I use, the words are:

I call to the Ancestors, those of the bloodline that have lost this their companion, gathering together as the hidden company, joining those who have come to say farewell and share their grief.
(BDO)

Calling to their gods for inspiration, those who have gathered are given the opportunity to share their memories, to express their love, honour, friendship and kinship, in music and poetry, in words of acknowledgement and thanks. The way in which this is done is often a beautiful portrayal of relationships, sometimes expressed in tender dignity and formality, and at other times through an exuberance of laughter, frustration, tears and rhythm. However they pour out, thanks are given for the life shared.

The bread and mead of the ritual feast might be substituted perhaps for a favourite food of the one who has died. The first part is offered back to the earth and the next to the one departed before the remainder is shared amongst all who have gathered. Some may be scattered and poured into the hole where the memorial tree is to be planted, or over the coffin, or (if inside the chapel) given into offering bowls to be used later, both by the priest and any others who wish to do so. Apples, traditionally the fruit of immortality, may also be used as feasting gifts.

Dusting the bread flour off her hands onto the black velvet of her skirt, she smiles at me, blinking, that smile of uncertainty from where the future is voided, washed away by a flood of tears. Returning to her place in the circle she looks down, acknowledging the strength I offer her, needing her solitude, and the words of the priest slip through the air like snow.

... 'in the tradition of our Ancestors it was understood that the soul travelled across the western ocean to the place of the sunset, diving then to the otherworldly Islands of Paradise that lie beneath the sea. There they rest, their spirits fed and nurtured, bathed in beauty and abundance, finding the healing they need before they return along the path of the Sun, through the darkness beneath the worlds, to rebirth with the rising Sun' ...

The sound of the harp fills the air and the cold flakes of snow-words become the softest white petals, falling to the damp earth of winter. The circle is quiet, eyes gazing at the ground. The deep hole is dark and open, the mud black, almost raw, the bread strangely white, scattered as if waiting as we listen to the harp, feeling it drift around us like a breeze in the mist.

The gathering is then given the opportunity to say their farewell to the soul who has died in whatever way this is felt appropriate. In Druidry, the gods of death might be invoked – 'You who ride the night with the Wild Hunt, gathering the souls of the departed, leading them along the hidden ways to Annwn, the place that is No Place, where they will rest until the time of their rebirth' – and prayers said for the one who has died, asking that they may find peace, joy and healing:

Death is merely that place where souls are detained only long enough to be sained with purifying smoke, fanned by the white wings of the sacred winds, til they are whiter than the swans of the songs, whiter than the seagull of the waves, whiter than the snow of the peaks, whiter than the pure love of heroes. Death is no oblivion, but a journey through cleansing, healing and change. We will meet again those whom we have loved. Such is the law of existence.
(BDO/CG)

As inspiration is called for, the ashes might be scattered, the body buried, the cairn built, the tree planted, or whatever is the focus of this particular rite. Using the traditional vision that the land of the dead lies across the western ocean, the place of the setting sun, many rites that honour those who have died are given a focus of the ocean. The lunar cycles that pull the tides add to this imagery, drawing many to celebrate and commemorate the dead in tune with the moon and the songs of the sea.

Feeling the flow of *awen*, its new creative energy, the rite comes to its close as each person is encouraged truly to let go, allowing the soul to make the rest of the journey, guided by those who greet him from the other worlds. The memories we have, the physicality of the memorial that has been erected or planted, are the gifts we are left with. Even when the sense of loss is overwhelming, these can guide us to honour the tidal flows of life, birth to death and rebirth again.

rituals for
INSPIRATION

THE festivals act as marker points that guide and support us through the cycle of the year, encouraging our adventure of growth and change. The rites of passage we celebrate are ways of using change positively, particularly those changes that life propels in our direction. This chapter is about using ritual to facilitate the changes we *choose* to make.

CLEARING THE FLOW

With every thought, every belief we hold, we create the world around us, not through some magical process but through our expectations and how those pattern the energy we express into the web of spirit connectedness. In theory, it is simple to identify those beliefs that are shaping our reality negatively and change them, so enabling us to create the world we would wish to live in. However, because our filing cabinet of belief systems is stored down in the subconscious mind, we are often not entirely clear as to *what* exactly is blocking the flow of positive energy and progressive intention. We know what we think, but we often deny what we actually believe.

The way that ritual works makes it a powerful tool for both identifying and re-prioritizing our attitudes and assumptions. Using imagery and sensation to slip into the subconscious, we can discover and dislodge those mud-drifts that are choking our ability both to access and to express our inspiration, so strengthening our creativity and reaching our exquisite freedom.

Once we have found a way of accessing our *awen* and been able to express it, offering our creativity as a gift back to the source of inspiration, the very nature of the *awen* energy and its inherent power clears the pathways. The process spirals, growing, intensifying, aching with its own need for perfection, for soul satisfaction. Yet how do we get started?

Finding Inspiration

However uninspired we feel in life, each of us has a knowing deep down as to where that pool of *awen* lies for us. Sources of inspiration are places and moments which we perceive as sacred and which are to us of exceptional beauty, soul to soul, spirit to spirit. It's not that we don't know what inspires us, but that we don't go there, we don't take the time, we don't think it is worth it or that we deserve it or ...

We might begin with a vague glimpse through heavy veils of denial that, yes, probably if we were to sit by the old beech on the hill and watch the sun rise over the fading lights of the city we'd feel better about life. Yet in truth if we were to follow that bright glimmer of a idea, allowing ourselves to be truly fed by the experience by opening up the gates of our barricades to the raw tenderness of our intimate space, revealing our soul's nakedness, we would feel more than a little 'better about life'. And if that were to happen, we might follow those bright shimmerings a little more often, and strangely, suddenly, there would be notions that would sparkle in other places too, energy glinting, our eyes slowly becoming accustomed to the vision of spirit beauty.

In honouring the spirits of place we are guided to locate ourselves physically, to know where we are and find our presence within our relationships there. Honouring the ancestors directs us to a presence in the flow of time, pausing in the moment between past and future, again allowing us to access the power of truly 'being'. As our relationship with the here-and-now grows, so does our sense of belonging, giving us enough confidence and certainty to use pro-actively and creatively the forces and energies evoked by the drives in our human soul, those of survival, sexuality and familiarity.

So we find sacred moments. Letting the defences of our body and mind relax, we relate, spirit to spirit. We share the energy of creation. Inspiration: the brilliance of being, knowing, doing, flowing, the energy of pure living filling our minds, undisturbed by our negative and negating defences.

THE MAGICAL PROCESS

Druidry is not a tradition that centres on magic. Magic might be defined as 'the art of consciously creating change by force of will'. In other words, a magical practice is one in which, having decided what we feel must happen, we acutely focus our energy and beliefs in order to adjust the web of spirit, effectively *making* it happen. While most who work magic have a strong ethical base and work in the main for healing, positive change and abundance, risks are always present. It is easy to impose our will, projecting our desires upon others, deluding ourselves as to what we really want or need. What might look like a blessing can turn into a curse. There's a fine line between the two when we are dealing with the power of will.

In Druidry, changes are made by reaching for inspiration, holding in our intention the problem, the crisis, sickness or scarcity we are dealing with. We are reaching for connection, to listen and to see clearly, to perceive the tangled threads of spirit, to touch the beauty and the power (even where it seems there is nothing but horror and devastation). We are questing our own confidence as we come into a state of perfect presence, where there is a congruence between our internal and external environment. We are calling for a harmony between our spirit and those spirits who dwell around us, above and below and within us.

When we find the source of *awen*, open to its flow and are balanced in our presence, its energy pours through us, inspiring us and fuelling us with a force that we *need* to express. We know suddenly what to do and we have the power to do it. Magic in Druidry is the creative release of *awen*, in tune with the spirit beauty that always surrounds us.

INTIMATE SPACE AND THE *NEMETON*

The art of knowing our intimate space is profoundly healing in itself. Claiming our own temple, a sanctuary of peace, the *nemeton* of intimate space is a circle we naturally stand in the centre of, finding strength and confidence. Yet it is at the edges that we grow and learn, dealing with what is just beyond our safe space, dealing with the scars and wounds, the build up of fear that is the expectation of repeating patterns.

The *nemeton*, then, is more than simply a sanctuary. It is by using the associations and connections we find on the edges of our sacred circle that we can discover and heal the crises which block our creative life flow. These associations are our relationships with the worlds we live in.

We may feel clear about the north being a place of death/rebirth, of night and winter, cold and dark, about the south being hot and golden with sunlight. Walking around the circle, beginning in the north west where the year ends, drawing us into the chaos of decay, we move into winter and then around the seasons – spring, summer, harvest/autumn. Yet this isn't an abrupt process in nature and neither should it be perceived as so in the circle. Feeling the slow natural shift is important. The same can be felt by walking the circle to feel the cycle of the day, allowing our imagination to pattern the changing light, minute by minute, upon each step of our journey. Walking through from birth in the north, around childhood into sexuality and through into our maturity and old age, we can also walk our lives, step by step, into the path of the circle's circumference. As we build more associations into the *nemeton*, we can place any tree or animal, place or moment of experience, vision of fantasy or desire upon the edges of our circle. So we allow the beliefs and memories of our subconscious mind to be painted, interconnectedly, across the canvas of our circle's rim.

In creating this clearly enough to have a confidence in its reality we gain a most powerful tool for divination and guidance, for addressing issues and finding solutions, for accessing inspiration. Gelling the associations can be done creatively by painting the circle on paper, drawing a wheel of correspondences, dancing it, singing it, and so on. The associations will change as we do, but a clear starting-point is useful.

Once this is done, we can use our circle in a ritual manner, either as part of a full ceremony or as a momentary pause. However, using the *nemeton* as such a tool enough times in a more formal way makes it easier to use it at the drop of a hat, in the midst of crisis when emotional currents are challenging our sanity and judgement. The process is held in the same way as other rites I have described. A simple summary would be:

- Centre inintimate space, the *nemeton*, balanced between earth and sky.
- Check the external location is accepting of the rite.
- Create the sacred circle, casting and consecrating.
- Honour the spirits of place and the ancestors.
- Clarify intention.

The intention in these rites would be the posing of the problem and the request to find a solution. If there is a good relationship with a specific deity or spirit of place, these can be invoked for guidance, but as the rite is about finding inspiration it is vital not to be blinkered in one direction.

The next step is to hold the intention clearly and locate it on the edge of the circle. It is important not to do this analytically but to hold the focus on the intention and simply to walk. Chanting, drumming or dancing can help, but only if they distract us from the talking-thinking self and guide us to meditate more fully on the problem. The subconscious mind, together with the spirits of our circle, will draw us to a particular place.

Locate the issue on the Circle's edge.
Explore the connection.

Whether we are looking outwards or towards the centre of the circle, as we explore the place we have come to, allowing all the connections and relationships to surface in our minds, the more open we are to the emotional and sensory impressions, the more we will gain. Facing the edge or not will have different effects, provoking us to feel more alert, defensive or vulnerable.

Many of the connections will be internal. Yet with eyes open, we can also look at the view of the physical world, letting this be a source of more clues and information.

Allowing emotion to intensify and letting ourselves slide into its flows of energy will take us deeper, bringing with it stronger impressions, reaching closer to the source of the problem. We might come face to face with a memory; we might plough right through it apocalyptically to emerge in a different stream, following a deeper feeling. Following these currents can take us out of the sanctuary of our *nemeton* and into another world. Such a course should only be taken by those who have the confidence, understanding and support to know that they can be held as they recover from such a journey. Such adventures made alone can leave us shaky, at best fragmented and without adequate reference points with which to integrate the experience into mundane reality.

Sometimes 'doorways' (in many guises) are offered us, though we may have to search carefully for them. They will take us out of the *nemeton* into surrounding worlds, offering us opportunities to consider the issue from an utterly different perspective.

What are these other worlds? Places of our subconscious mind, memories of past lives, realms of faerie, of elemental energy, of myth, they are as real as we wish them to be, as real as we allow them to be, and their effect on us is relative to how we perceive them. They are not places to journey through lightly, requiring clarity of mind, quick and sharp wit, and an understanding of the power of thought, intention, expectation and desire. Above all, it should never be assumed in these realms that those we meet are what they seem, nor that they are working for our best interests. These worlds are a place of learning, soul deep.

In whatever way we explore the connection between the problem posed and the time and space we find ourselves in, analysing it too quickly can take us out of any beneficial space. Simply by letting the impression wash through us and allowing ourselves to respond naturally, intuitively, emotionally, we will learn the most. Putting the pieces together is something to do later, after the journey is done and we have returned to the centre.

Discovering the connections can be profoundly revealing or utterly baffling. Either way, the next part of the rite is to call for inspiration. Holding the rite's intention clearly once more, we reach for clarity, by chanting the *awen* or invoking a spirit or deity who would guide the way. It may be that staying in just the same place in our circle is appropriate. It may be that in the search for *awen* we are led to another place. If necessary, spending a little time understanding the place that we have been brought to can be useful.

If we have become accustomed to the glint of inspiration, we will know what to look for. If still we are struggling to perceive the spirit beauty that is the expression of divine creative power, we can only work on losing the expectations of our thinking mind, being open, awake, watching, waiting ...

It can come instantly, quicker than a blink. It may take a long while, our mind drifting and releasing simply to observe and feel again and again. It may explode like a flash of light, like a mouthful of sweet lemon juice. It may slide into our perception, an adder curling its smooth dark muscles around our open stretch, moonlight gleaming off its coils. It brings a moment that is both profoundly peaceful yet exquisitely exhilarating.

Using the circle to help us find inspiration, our subconscious and *nemeton* spirits guide us physically, turning us in the direction in which we need to look, presenting us with a collage of resources, trees, animals, elementals, landscapes and memories in which reside myriad spirits of place, powers of nature, deities, dragons and more. If we let them show us, opening our eyes in trust, held in our *nemeton*, we will see.

Call for Inspiration.
Recentre, integrate, give Thanks and Close.

Whether we use the inspiration then and there, solving the problem, scribbling down the solution, grabbing the paintbrush, flute or journal, or we take it with us from the circle to be implemented in real time, before we leave its consecrated space we must recentre. Walking back to the middle, balancing again consciously between earth and sky, we rework our initial intention, to take the solution with us. It is our declaration, our statement of change, and one we hold with us until the appropriate actions have been taken.

Where the change to be made is the reprioritizing of basic beliefs, shifting core attitudes and constructs about our world, the new intention made in this rite can become a clear and usable affirmation. Effective affirmations should be a short phrase (five or six words at most) in the present tense and positive, such as: 'I am free to be me', 'My words are of value' or 'I am cared for.' These are phrases that become a part of daily life, a hum on the bus, a sign on the mirror, a chant in the shower. They are phrases which over time we learn to carry with us everywhere, guiding us to react and expect and assume in an entirely different way.

Sometimes the change required cannot be adequately done in the rite for inspiration yet it needs a ritual framework. Here the structure of a rite of passage laid out in Chapter Ten can be used, honouring the past, accepting the present and walking with courage into a new future. The affirmation statement can be a central part of this rite, urging us to adjust our behaviour, to move on into freedom, personal power and love.

THE POWER OF THE MOON

While rites for inspiration and change can be done at any time, the energies of the wider moment can act as a potent fuel and an effective guide, and it is for this reason that the lunar cycles are honoured in Druidry and native spiritual traditions around the world.

An extraordinarily lush trackway of self-realization and self-acceptance, the moon cycles wake us to the tides and flows of our own energy. Women in their fertile years may have more overt signs of the fluid and hormonal changes evoked by the lunar tides, reflected in ovulation and menstruation, with all the related physical and emotional effects, but these changes of push and pull work equally through the bodies of post-fertile women, men and children. The waxing time that takes us to fullness and the waning time that brings us back into the dark draw us up into growth and back into decay in just the same way that spring's opening and autumn's receding guide us through the temperate year.

The moon's force is considered not as strong as the heat of the sun, which creates its exquisite art of seasonal change. Its tremendous power moves the flows of the oceans, of blood, of emotions, but still it is considered not so obviously to affect the world by its journey. Yet, because the moon's cycle takes around 29 days, not 365, the useable qualities of these tides are much more freely available. As they move faster, we can learn better from them, guiding ourselves to flow in their rhythm, accept their effect and work with that to our advantage.

Different Druids celebrate different phases of the moon, not only according to the style of their practice but also because of individual cravings and strengths. Classical texts tell us that Druids worked at the quarter points when the moon was a perfect half. Many now celebrate the lunar tide by acknowledging the moon's power when she is full, when the Earth glides directly between the light of the sun and the rock of the moon. Others gather when the moon is dark, moving across the other side between the Earth and sun, whose energies together accentuate the gravitational pull, intensifying the force. Some find the lunar tide most inspiring at that point when the slightest crescent gives a glimmer of anticipation in a new cycle ahead. The old Scots Gaelic prayer for the new moon can be heard at these rites:

Hail to thee, thou new moon
Beauteous guidant of the sky
Hail to thee, thou new moon
Beauteous fair one of grace

Hail to thee, thou new moon
Beauteous guidant of the stars
Hail to thee, thou new moon
Beauteous loved one of my heart

Hail to thee, thou new moon
Beauteous guidant of the clouds
Hail to thee, thou new moon
Beauteous dear one of the heavens!
(CG)

Creating ritual for the lunar holy days is about exploring the depth and value of our relationship with the sacred moon, discovering how its gravity moves the tides of our bodies, affecting our souls, enthralling the streams of our water and blood, our hormones and the flows of our emotional energy. It is about working with that natural process, catching the wave and surrendering to its power, like ocean surfing ...

The framework of a lunar ritual might be formal or have the ease of a close relationship. As moon rites, like any rites of change and inspiration, tend to be intense and emotional affairs, the circle is often cast tightly, allowing an intimate space for the process of learning, growth and self-expression. As the spirits of place are honoured in the ritual, we bear in mind the effect of the moment's distinctive power, blessed by the moon's reflected sunlight or the darkness of the skies. As moon rites are usually done at night, the stars, distant suns, are also honoured.

CHALLENGE: *what is the time?*

Whether the ideas and understandings about the moment at which the ritual is being held are spoken aloud or not depends on who is gathered together and how much needs to be declared so that everyone is moving along the same track. First, we look to the phase of the moon.

When the moon is waxing, showing its right side with reflected sunlight through the afternoon and the first half of the night, the tide is rising. Any ceremony done at this time is energizing, drawing us out of ourselves into creativity and expression. It is a time of making when we seek inspiration as to how we can better create the worlds we live in. With the first crescent we find new life and we nurture this as the moon swells with light.

At the moon's fullness, we have a sense of completion, yet just as at Alban Hefin when the sun reaches his zenith there is here too a point of turning. The sun and moon draw us in different directions, their opposing energy alive with attraction and confrontation. It is a time of excitement, filled with the tension of expressing our creativity, which rises to a climax as the peak moment comes, bringing with it relief and manifestation.

The waning moon is the time of releasing, of letting go into the decay and death that bring us the freedom of living in spirit. We see the left side of the moon in its receding state during the second half of the night and through the morning. It teaches us of drawing inwards, of dissolving and contracting. It is a time of cleaning up and clearing out, cutting away the dross, of positive destruction.

When the moon reaches its darkness and is lost to us for three long days, its power is at its strongest, magnified and intensified by the sun behind it. Our focus is internal, in a place of inner knowing, as we lie in the dark womb of nature's creation. Ritual at this time is potent, surging, uncompromising, as our souls move through the nightscape of dreams, connected through our roots to the great mother of all life.

When we look to the moment at which the rite takes place, we also look at which moon we are honouring. There are 12 to 13 in each solar year and each one reflects the qualities of the natural world over which its energy flows, as velvety soft and richly sumptuous as sap.

There are written lists of associations, tables of magical correspondences, which inform us of the different qualities of each ripening and darkening moon. Yet our perception is so much about our own personal relationship, human spirit to moon spirit, that – except as a source of inspiration – anybody else's visions are often wholly irrelevant. By creating our own lunar calendar we reveal those deep internal rivers, patterns of our worlds and our psyche that guide us as we journey through the darkness of our soul, the darkness of the night.

Around Samhain, as the wheel of the year comes to its changing point, find the information you need for the following cycle, then check which moons overlap with the four seasonal festivals of Calan Gaeaf/Samhain, Gwyl Forwyn/Imbolc, Calan Mai/Beltane and Gwyl Awst/Lughnasadh. Then name these moons. You can use names which others have used or create your own, the important issue being that the names used accurately reflect what is happening at this time in the natural world around you. For me in southern England these moons are:

Winter begins at Calan Gaeaf with Leaf Dance Moon.
Spring begins at Gwyl Forwyn with White Waking Moon.
Summer begins at Calan Mai with White Lady Moon.
Harvest begins at Gwyl Awst with Claim Song Moon.

The trees are stripped by the Cailleach in Leaf Dance Moon. The wild snowdrops open through White Waking, the hawthorn blooms with White Lady's tide, the grain harvest begins as Claim Song swells.

There are two moons in between each of the festivals, making 12 moons in total. The solar festivals of the Albans fit into these. Name these moons, too, taking note that every few years another moon sneaks in, balancing our year. This thirteenth moon is a magical tide, if not always an easy one. It is often called the Quickening Moon.

Once our moons are named, as each next tide comes, we can add to our understanding of it, filling in associations that work for ourselves, mirroring and honouring the spirits who live in the world around us. During certain moons, trees will flower or unfurl their leaves, offer their berries or fruit. At certain times, flowers will shine, glowing in the moonlight as if this is their special time, their magical healing energies brimming with the moon's vibration. Animals play during certain moons, the rabbits, hares, fox and badgers of our wild landscape; birds nest, sing, listen to us, flock and dance high in the skies.

Astrologers will connect the energy qualities of the constellations through which the moons pass, together with the quality of the sun's light that it reflects. Knowing this, we can perhaps learn more deeply what the moment offers us as potential. In this way we can see that, for example, White Lady Moon is around the time when the sun is moving in front of the stars that make up the constellation Taurus, an astrological 'fixed earth' sign that focuses on physicality. The full moon of Taurus passes before Scorpio, a 'fixed water' sign that acts as a doorway to deep wells of emotion. The combination is a powerful one to those who have an awareness and understanding of the energies involved.

The cycle of moons that I might use with their sacred trees and plants is this:

Leaf Dance Moon of the Blackthorn and Ivy
Fire Friend Moon of the Yew and Holly
Star Frost Moon of the Mistletoe and Winter Aconite
(Quickening Moon of the Rowan and Stinking Hellebore)
White Waking Moon of the Birch and Snowdrop
Wind Tossed Moon of the Willow and Stitchwort
Flower Shower Moon of the Ash and Celandine
White Lady Moon of the Hawthorn and Columbine
Bright Love Moon of the Oak and Wild Rose
Field Poppy Moon of the Maple and Poppy
Claim Song Moon of the Hazel and St John's Wort
Still Green Moon of the Apple and Mugwort
Blood Berry Moon of the Elder and Bramble

Having a clear idea of both the phase of the moon and the qualities of the particular moon we are honouring, we can weave these into the intention of our lunar ritual, using the whole environment as we perceive it as a teacher and guide in our ritual practice.

Honouring the Power, the lunar deity and/or spirits of nature.

Whether we call to a named god or goddess or use a generic term, because these rites are focused upon the spirit and energy of the moon, it is important that we understand and honour the spirit to which we are talking.

Spirit to spirit, our relationship can develop in the same way that any does, exploring and strengthening bonds of trust so that we might relax our circle of intimate space, allowing the moon's potent energy to flow through us more fully, inspiring change and growth. As in any relationship, there are many other spirits whose energy affects and influences the world through which we reach to touch each other, soul deep; as we stretch within ourselves, reaching for the moon, our fingers move through the spirits of the trees, the stories of our ancestral kin, the cloud folk and the energy of so many stars. By honouring the spirits of place, those who witness our actions, our relationship can find support to grow still further.

The Quest, *Awen*, weaving spirit with spirit.
The Focus, intention, creativity and change.
The Celebration and Feasting.

In lunar rites, our whole being is reaching through and for the intuitive and emotional within ourselves. It is even more effective in these rites, then, to allow the energy to swirl and twist and find its own course as we call for inspiration. Chanting or sounding (non-verbal vocalization of emotion or energy) is an excellent way of doing this. A chant need not be of a formal phrase or word – any line that comes to mind or words that are appropriate can be equally compelling and transforming, the rhythm and tone being as pivotal as the words. So long as we realize that what is chanted will be absorbed deeply into the subconscious mind and should therefore be a positive or directive statement, not a negative, then we can't go wrong. The effectiveness of simple sound without words, of freeing the voice just to express the energy flowing through us, can bring exquisite results that easily reveal just how powerful this medium can be. Using music and drums, movement and dance can further deepen the effect.

A good deal of the process and its success is about letting go the inhibitions that compromise our creativity. As we seek for inspiration, diving into a chant or rhythm, we are freeing our perception to see the world differently, to see ourselves differently, guided by sound and not by thought or reason. The landscape around us becomes as music: spirit energy in motion, in creative flow. In the potentiality of the ever-shifting moving fluidity of it all, we seek out the brilliance and beauty that is our *awen*.

Celebration of the moment, whether it be every dark phase of every moon or the delicious feeling of being with friends gathered especially for the last night of waxing, as we work our lunar rites in the Druid tradition we are calling to the spirit of our beautiful moon. Whether the moon is a deep well of our own inspiration or simply a guide, directing our path, we are reaching to make a conscious connection with that which has power over the great oceans of our planet and the tides of our emotion. Aching to deepen our relationship, spirit to spirit, we bring to the moon our rites of change so that we might be inspired, so that its energy might shimmer through our growing and our releasing, our living and our loving.

THE POWER OF LOVE

The motivation to perform a ritual for change, whether one of making or releasing, is most often prompted by a sense of not having enough, not being good enough. Through our feeling of lack, we start to fantasize of more, often unaware of the underlying beliefs that are maintaining our perception of 'not enough'. Of course, often our world is indeed in need of change, for what we lack is confidence, freedom, health or understanding, and we are madly struggling, body and soul, to reach a better state of living. Sometimes it is a physical crisis, sometimes a problem in our vision of the world we live in, or in our self-perception. Sometimes there is no lack at all, except in our understanding.

When we feel in need of a rite of change, we have usually already asked what it is that we want. We might even believe we know what must change and would be more than happy to impose our will upon the threads of the web that connect us in order to force the change into manifestation. Yet in the Druid tradition this temptation is resisted; our view may be clouded by projections, reflections, veiled lusts and hidden fears. So the Druid will instead seek out inspiration. Using his knowledge of the cycles of nature, the seasons of the Earth, the path of the sun, the tides of the moon, the Druid searches for the deeper meaning behind the wanting.

The answer comes again and again back to relationship.

Where we are craving a rite of making, a way of assuring or affirming our journey out of scarcity and into abundance, it is our connection with the spirits of place that is out of kilter. The spirits of the land who feed, clothe and shelter us, the spirits of the skies who offer us breath, light, warmth and freedom, the spirits of the seas that cleanse and guide us through the tides and cycles of life, these will always listen to those who honour them, who respect their power and seek to listen to their wisdom. In developing our relationship with the essence of creation, we find a level of interaction that inspires trust, easing the tension that is inherent in the drive for survival.

Trust is pivotal, too, where our rite of change is focused on shifting out of a situation in which we are feeling a lack of recognition, status, value and respect. Whether our crisis is being expressed through work colleagues, through friendships or closer relationships, it is the interaction, soul to soul, that is unbalanced or blocked. As so much of our understanding of relationship is taught us by our parents, their parents in turn passing down their parents' wit, wisdom and mistakes, connecting better with our ancestors, those in spirit whose stories linger in our DNA and drift in the air we breathe, and those in body, beginning with our parents, is a crucial part of creating change in that part of our life.

Rites of change performed to invoke healing are concerned with negative energy that has built up, whether inside a person, a house or building, a piece of land or body of water. The craft of cleansing a body or place of the emotional negativity is also about relationship. As often as not, where we perceive 'negative' energy, we are simply experiencing the friction where souls cannot move in harmony. We paste the label of 'negative' onto something or someone to whom we cannot relate. Where there is decay and destruction, a situation that is in a process of breakdown, we perceive it as negative and, scared of its power, we try to heal it, to hold it together. Yet often the falling apart is a natural and necessary part of the life–death cycle of existence.

The fine lines between negativity that is 'real' and negativity that is our projected fear or perception are usually blurred. By seeking inspiration about the situation, we can learn where the lines lie and not waste energy or disrespect a spirit's creative process just because to us it looks horrendous or feels 'wrong'.

So, a rite of change, and indeed any ritual, is about enhancing relationship. Finding our centre, balanced between Earth and sky, powerful within the *nemeton* of our own sacred space, we turn to the threads that connect us, spirit to spirit, with all of creation. There, in our search for freedom, for joy and satisfaction, we find blocks of mistrust, constraining our ability to live as we would wish. We seek inspiration, eager to clear the problems, perceiving the world as sacred, finding beauty where before we saw only dull grey apathy, and through the energy of *awen* we heal and strengthen our understanding of intimacy. Our ability to make a relationship that is meaningful grows and increasingly we are nourished by our interaction with all creation. The energy flows through us more clearly with each tide. We are able to give more and we open to receive more, diving deeper, gliding higher, trusting.

This is love. Devoid of the sticky rough clasp-holds of need, inspired by a brilliance that is the shining energy of *awen*, spirit to spirit, beautiful, we trust sufficiently to be open, naked in our intimacy, invulnerable and tender. Our creativity flows, a wild river of freedom that courses between such lush fertile shores, laughing with joy, shining with ecstasy, the clear waters of sweet appreciation.

LIVING RITUAL

Whatever the ritual, our goal is to drink from the cup of *awen*. Inspired, in a world that is sacred, we start to live life to the full, honouring the powers of nature so that each step is a prayer, each breath another line of the story we will leave behind us. Learning, growing, finding our soul nourishment, the world we live in is our own creativity.

Ritual is a concentrated moment of that living.

Ritual

going DEEPER

THE ESSENCE OF RITUAL

Ritual is that pause which is the moment when we move from the natural swirls and surges of life into the sanctuary of the sacred circle. There our focus is intentionally directed, our thoughts concentrated, our experience and actions acutely enhanced, before the barriers dissolve again and we slip back into the free currents of creation. The ritual circle is like a training place where we focus on life, issue by issue, carefully stepping for a moment, stone to stone, clearing our perception, profoundly aware. Dismissing life's distractions, we bring our attention to the search for inspiration, waking ourselves to see the world as inspirited and sacred. From the conscious focus of ritual, then, we take our skills and sacred vision back into our lives, to live more consciously, competently, effectively.

The fine arts of appreciation and respect are central to living in a sacred manner. That doesn't mean ingratiation and grovelling, but standing centred, listening and *hearing*, watching and *seeing*, working to offer the height of our soul creativity into the worlds within which we live. The ability to make good relationships, to grasp the nature of love, to share, to trust and, when appropriate, to bow and turn away, these are often given us in the twisted form of patterns of miscommunication passed through countless generations. Yet they are skills that are as much a part of living with integrity as any religious practice. In honouring the environment around us and within us, we dance within the perfect flow of life's creative energy.

As we deepen our relationship with those that inspire us – the oak in the breeze, the moon on the ocean, the musician's waterfall of rich harmonies, our lover with blue eyes, our valley home – honouring the spirit source of *awen*, our inspiration grows, as does our creativity.

As Druidry is an oral tradition, the ideas in this book are not offered as a liturgy to follow. Pictures, possibilities and traditions are described in order to show the potential of ritual. It is a treasure box to explore, filled with tools and resources, paint and paper, scissors and glue. If each one of us honours our individuality, our own perception of the land and our own inheritance, what we do with what we find in that box will reveal our sacred and unique vision.

BE THE *AWEN*

It seems appropriate to end the book honouring a wild soul who, in the drizzling rain of a Seattle morning, up in northwest America, affirmed for me the beauty of individual creativity and the power of laughter, as ritual ...

His eyes are sparkling. His grin spreads wider than his face should allow, reaching out into the colours of the wind that dance around us, wet and cold, fresh with the mountain air of the passing storm. I'm shivering, tired after a long sleepless night, and he looks at me, like a young child, so eager to give yet scared of the intimacy that might evoke.

'I'd like to share with you,' he whispers. 'I think this is a good time.' And he looks at the others who are shivering with me, my partner and a mutual friend who raises his eyebrows, anticipating, half smiling.

'What would you like to share?' I ask.

'Well,' he frowns, 'this ... this just feels like the perfect moment for a ritual. Know what I mean?'

'Oh, abso-bloomin'-lutely,' my partner smiles and sighs as our eyes meet. It's been a long trip and the flight home is a matter of hours away. I look around at the forest of hemlock and birch, its branches dripping with moss and rain.

'This rite is called the Rite of Five Quarters.'

We hold hands, the four of us, a damp circle on the mud and broken stones of the trackway by the car, and for a moment there is stillness. My heart slips slowly into the rhythm of the others' breath, the wash of the wind upon the wide hill-side. I can feel the birds sheltering in the trees, the sound of the fire and the drums from the clearing where the native peoples gather, the stories of the land shimmering, waiting, always waiting to be heard. I feel the footfalls of bobcats who have walked this way and my mind moves in the circle of its horizon, every sense in my body open to perceive, watching, waiting, listening to the stillness. The calm is humming, flowing through me like an old river. It's exquisite.

He lets go of my hand and I open my eyes. He smiles, listening to words not spoken, and reaches into his pocket. Holding out his hand, he softly places something into each of ours.

He says softly, 'A quarter for you … a quarter for you…' I open my fingers. It's a little silver coin. 'A quarter for you…' My partner is already laughing. 'And a quarter for me.' His grin is radiant, like an unquestionable statement, inflexible and proud, the little boy looking out from far inside.

'And…?' I ask.

'And,' he nods, one eyebrow raised, 'a quarter back to the Mother.' And he hurls the last coin up into the air, through the cool wind and rain, through the tangle of the old trees. My mind flies with it, wild and free, breathing in life.

'May we be the *awen*,' he whispers.

And my feet softly touch the ground.

finðing more
RESOURCES

 IT is too easy to resort to others' words and forget first to search for our own. The best store of resources for our ritual treasure box is the natural world, the raw beauty of nature not yet analysed or processed. Walking through the forest, on the moors, across the hills, meandering through the city park, gazing out across the sea, ideas for ritual will come from the same spirit beauty that is our well of inspiration.

Words in Print

Books are offerings of other people's creativity. None are objective fact, neither do they give an authentic doctrine, for there is no 'authenticity', simply the reality of creation, evolving through time, touched by so many souls in their search for freedom.

Principles of Druidry (Thorsons, 1998) is my own introduction to the tradition.
Spirits of the Sacred Grove (Thorsons, 1998) offers my personal vision of the cycle of the festivals, of rites of passage and spiritual growth, from the perspective of a Druid priestess.
A Guide to Druidry by Philip Shallcrass (Piatkus, 2000) is another introduction to the tradition, with a good section on myths and how they weave into the seasonal cycle.
The Stations of the Sun by Ronald Hutton (Oxford University Press, 1996) gives comprehensive and readable research into the traditions, history and folklore of the British festival cycle.
The Druid Renaissance by Philip Carr-Gomm (ed.) (Thorsons, 1996) is a wonderful collection

of articles by Druids from the spectrum of the tradition, giving ideas for further associations, sources of learning and forms of practice.

Exploring the World of the Druids by Miranda Green (Thames & Hudson, 1998) is a richly illustrated history of Druidry from the earliest records to the present day, setting out the evidence for ritual practice. The history is excellent, but some details about modern practice are inaccurate.

Carmina Gadelica by Alexander Carmichael (Floris Books, 1992) is a collection of hymns and incantations gathered in the Highlands of Scotland in the nineteenth century and well used by all those interested in the old native traditions.

A Modern Herbal by Mrs M. Grieve (Penguin Books, 1978) includes the history and folklore of medicinal plants as well as detailed information on preparation, dosages, constituents and effects.

The Complete Book of Incense, Oils and Brews by Scott Cunningham (Llewellyn, 1991) is a comprehensive magical guide.

Cattern Cakes and Lace by Julia Jones and Barbara Deer (Dorling Kindersley, 1987) is a beautiful book of recipes for festivals and occasions through the year.

Wild Food by Roger Phillips (Pan, 1983) is a delicious book about identifying, gathering, preparing and cooking wild plants and fungi that takes any reader into a deep connection with the local landscape.

William Morris publishes a *Lunar Tree Calendar* which is an exquisitely creative and comprehensive resource, giving festival details, astrological information and clear images of the changing tides of the moon. Available from good stores or Edge of Time, BCM Edge, London WC1N 3XX, England. Website: http://freepages.pavilion.net/users/william/

Contacts

The British Druid Order (BDO) is the growing international Druid order for which I work. It publishes texts and journals, holds public rites, workshops and other events, guides private practice and maintains a network of individuals and Groves. Full ceremonies are available from the office for marriages and funerals, and priests can be contacted.

PO Box 29, St Leonards-on-Sea, East Sussex, TN37 7YP, England
Website: http://www.druidorder.demon.co.uk

The Order of Bards, Ovates and Druids is a large international Druid order offering a basic correspondence course in Druidry. It has a strong network of individuals and Groves.

PO Box 1333, Lewes, East Sussex, BN7 3ZG, England
Website: http://www.druidry.org

The Guild of Soul Midwives is an organization specializing in rites of the dying and for death. It offers a training course and acts as a network for celebrants who can take people through the whole process of a soul's departure.

BCM Soul Midwives, London WC1N 3XX, England

LifeRites is an organization with no specific religious framework but a deeply spiritual foundation. It offers information and guidance on all rites of passage and has a network of priests. There is a sound training course for those wishing to act as celebrants. Fees and conditions are clearly laid out.

PO Box 101, Aldershot, Hampshire, GU11 3UN, England
Website: http://www.liferites.org

INDEX

 Ritual

Index

215

 Ritual

Pretannic Isles 19
problem-solving 195–7
puberty, rite 176, 179

Qabbala 76
quest 22–3
Quickening Moon 201, 202

relationships:
  and change 205–6
  making 207–8
  see also spirit-to-spirit
  relationships
reproduction 8
respect 207
responsibility, as tool 56
retirement 187
Rhiannon 148
rites of passage 164–90
ritual:
  art of 5
  definition 3–4, 7–10, 29
  essence of 207–8
  robes 63–4
  Romans, influence 16
  roots 15–20

sacred, definition 5
sacred energy, exchange
  of 24
sacred space 48–61
safety, in ritual 9, 29, 105

and children 174
  and location 51
St John's Day 151
Samhain 122–9, 201
Samhuinn 122
sanctuary, inner 55–7, 79
seasons 43, 118–20
secular rites 165
settings 48–61
sex 8, 9, 15
  first experience, rite
  179–80
shelter 109–11
Sky Lord 149, 150
solstices:
  in earlier ritual 121
  megalithic markers 120
  see also Alban festivals
soul creativity 21–3
sounding 203–4
space, *see* sacred space
spirit:
  definition 4
  perception 6
  power of 6
  and the sacred 5
spirit essence 4
Spirit of the Old Year,
  burning 127
spirit-to-spirit relationships 6, 8
  and *awen* 23–4
  deepening 117

and healing 115–17
  and inspiration 192–3
  in lunar rituals 203
spirits of the four
  directions 86–7, 97–8
spirits of place 192
  and altars 109
  and healing 116–17
  in rituals 19, 36–7
  three worlds 87–8, 97
  see also ancestors;
  guardian spirits; house
  spirits
spirituality, native 19–20
spring 201
Spring Equinox 141–6
staffs, wooden 72
standing stones 60, 120
Star Frost Moon 202
Still Green Moon 202
stone circles 51, 60–1
  historical use 15
  megalithic markers 120
stone people, *see* devas
Stonehenge 48–9, 50
stones:
  carved 60
  as tools 67–8
  see also standing stones;
  stone circles
stories 39–43
subconscious 113, 191
  and intention 35, 195

Thorsons

Directions for life

www.thorsons.com

The latest mind, body and spirit news

Exclusive author interviews

Read extracts from the latest books

Join in mind-expanding discussions

Win great prizes every week

Thorsons catalogue & ordering service

www.thorsons.com